Monticello

A GUIDEBOOK

A GUIDEBOOK

Thomas Jefferson Foundation

Charlottesville, Virginia

CONTENTS

This book was made possible by support from the Martin S. and Luella Davis Publications Endowment.

H G F E D C

ISBN 1-882886-04-6

Thomas Jefferson by Charles Willson Peale, 1791.

"I have heard my father say
that when quite a boy the top of this
mountain was his favorite retreat, here
he would bring his books to study, here
[he] would pass his holiday and leisure
hours: that he never wearied of
gazing on the sublime and beautiful
scenery that spread around."

MARTHA JEFFERSON RANDOLPH

JEFFERSON'S
Monticello

Susan R. Stein
Curator

T he center of Thomas Jefferson's private world was Monticello, the house and 5,000-acre plantation which occupied his attention and imagination for more than fifty years. The exceptional house, ornamented by extensive gardens and surrounded by working farms, was designed entirely by Jefferson, who supervised its construction and expansion from 1768 until virtually the end of his life.

Monticello was home not only to Jefferson and his large family but also to as many as 135 slaves who worked the plantation's four farms, helped construct the house and outbuildings, and labored to perform the requisite household tasks. Jefferson's world was focused here.

"…all my wishes end where I hope my days will end, at Monticello."

THOMAS JEFFERSON

Monticello was Jefferson's retreat from the "hated occupations of politics" that drew him away from his family, his farm, and his books. Especially after his retirement, Monticello was the place where Jefferson could enjoy "the circle of our nearest connections." He was also free, at last, to follow "the tranquil pursuits of science," studying astronomy and the natural world around him.

Jefferson sketch for the first Monticello.

BUILDING THE HOUSE

The First Monticello

When he came of age in 1764, Jefferson inherited about 3,000 acres in Albemarle County from his father, the surveyor Peter Jefferson (1708-1757). Jefferson later selected a portion of this land for the site of his new dwelling, calling it "Monticello" (little mountain in old Italian). The mountain he chose rose 560 feet above the Rivanna River and had been a favorite place since boyhood. In May 1768, at the age of twenty-five, he began to level the already gentle top of the mountain.

> *"I have here but one room, which, like the cobler's, serves me for parlour, for kitchen and hall. I may add, for bed chamber and study too."*
>
> THOMAS JEFFERSON, 1771

After a fire in 1770 destroyed the family dwelling at nearby Shadwell and most of his belongings, Jefferson moved to a single room on the mountaintop, in what is now the South Pavilion. He brought his bride Martha Wayles Skelton (1748?-1782) to the same small dwelling in January 1772.

Jefferson's design for Monticello was influenced by his

understanding of architecture, which came chiefly from books. An accomplished classical scholar, Jefferson admired ancient architecture, writing that "Roman taste, genius, and magnificence excite ideas." He studied the work of Andrea Palladio (1508-1580), the renowned Italian Renaissance proponent of a universal architectural vocabulary based upon the architecture of ancient Rome. Jefferson owned five editions of Palladio's famous *Quattro Libri,* which illustrated the architectural orders, construction methods, and buildings of Rome. Jefferson was said to have called it his "Bible."

Jefferson applied his knowledge of architecture to the design of Monticello, and Monticello's distinction was quickly recognized by visitors. His ambitious plan called for double-storied porticoes on the east and west fronts. The east portico served as the entry into a lodge, with stairs located in rooms on either side. The parlor, with its octagonal bay, was west of the hall, and

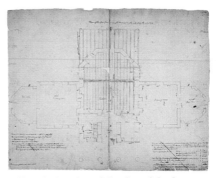

Jefferson's drawing of the plan of the first Monticello, 1770s.

above it, on the second floor, a library. Octagonal bays also terminated the room adjoining the dining room on the north and Jefferson's bed chamber on the south.

Work proceeded slowly on the first house and was halted in 1784; Jefferson himself reported in 1796 that it was "never more than half finished." Just how much of the first house was completed is not precisely known, although it appears that the exterior was mostly finished. The interior brick walls may never have been plastered.

Jefferson called the Maison Carrée in Nîmes "the best morsel of ancient architecture now remaining." Detail of the Maison Carrée, the Arena and the Tour Magne at Nîmes *by Hubert Robert, 1787.*

European Influence on Jefferson's Architecture

After the death of his wife in 1782, Jefferson resumed public service. In 1784, he embarked for France, where he served as a trade commissioner and later as Minister. In Paris, Jefferson was excited by the new architecture of the Palais Royal, Halle aux Bleds (grain market), and especially the Hôtel de Salm (now the Museum of the Legion of Honor), a fashionable new residence with a dome.

Jefferson's enthusiasm for classical architecture was also stimulated by what he saw in Europe. On a trip through France in 1787, he reported to a friend that he was "nourished with the remains of Roman grandeur." Jefferson was exhilarated by the Maison Carrée, the first-century A.D. Roman temple in Nîmes, which had served as the basis of his design for the Virginia State Capitol in Richmond in 1785.

In the fall of 1789, Jefferson returned to America with his daughters Martha and Maria and in March 1790, joined the federal government at its headquarters in New York. After serving nearly four years as Secretary of State,

Jefferson was eager to retire from the political arena and return to Monticello.

The Second Monticello

Jefferson's plans to enlarge Monticello from eight to twenty-one rooms were well advanced when he returned home in January 1794. The prolonged building process, often delayed by Jefferson's long absences, would not be essentially complete until 1809, the year that he retired from the presidency. The upper story was removed and the northeast front extended. Monticello would double in size with the addition of passageways and rooms alongside them on three levels. (See plan on page 20 showing first and second Monticellos.)

"I am going to Virginia... I am then to be liberated from the hated occupations of politics, and to remain in the bosom of my family, my farm, and my books. I have my house to build, my fields to farm, and to watch for the happiness of those who labor for mine."

THOMAS JEFFERSON, 1793

The improved Monticello incorporated many architectural features that Jefferson had admired in France—double-height public rooms, a dome, bed alcoves, skylights, indoor privies, cisterns for collecting water, and narrow staircases.

View of the west front of Monticello, by Jane Braddick Peticolas, 1825.

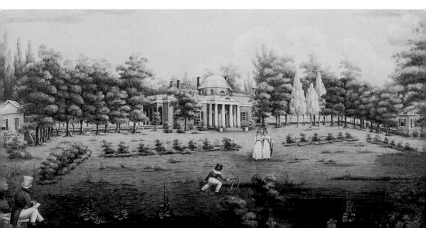

Many innovations reflected Jefferson's pursuit of comfort and convenience—double-acting doors connecting the Entrance Hall and Parlor, a dumbwaiter to carry wine from the wine cellar to the Dining Room, Venetian blinds between the columns of the southwest portico to provide shade, a clothes pole in his closet, and enclosed verandas adjoining the Greenhouse.

As Jefferson added modern features to Monticello, he also amplified its neoclassical vocabulary. The designs for the ornamental decoration were derived from many different Roman buildings that Jefferson had studied in two important architectural books in his library, *Parallele de l'Architecture Antique avec la Moderne* (1764-66) by Fréart de Chambray and Jombert's edition of *Les Edifices Antiques de Rome* (1779) by Antoine Desgodetz. The Temple of Fortuna Virilis inspired the ornamentation of his Bed Chamber; the Temple of Jupiter the Thunderer, his Parlor. The Apollo, or sun god frieze of the North Piazza was drawn from the Baths of Diocletian. The distinctive griffins of the Entrance Hall were derived from those of the Temple of Antoninus and Faustina in Rome.

Opposite: Jefferson's Bed Chamber. Above: Drawing of the frieze of the Temple of Fortuna Virilis.

The Expansion of Monticello

Preparations for Monticello's expansion began in 1792 when Jefferson ordered window sashes from Philadelphia and his slaves began to quarry limestone for mortar. Construction began in earnest in 1796 with the removal of the stone columns on the northeast facade and the excavation of the cellars. Parts of the existing house were carefully demolished in an effort to salvage bricks for reuse.

Monticello's construction was carried out by a group of experienced hired workmen and Jefferson's slaves, who lived on Mulberry Row, the principal plantation "street." Slaves dug the cellars, hauled limestone, felled and transported trees, sawed lumber, manufactured nails, and learned much about the trades of the hired workmen. Some became highly skilled craftsmen themselves. Burwell Colbert, a butler, was trained as a painter and glazier, and Jupiter, a manservant and groom, was a stone-cutter. With instruction from David Watson and later James Dinsmore, the slave John Hemings became an accomplished joiner who produced fine furniture.

Jefferson located skilled workmen who came from distant places to practice their trades. The superior quality of Monticello's workmanship is attributable not only to Jefferson's determination but also to the talents of Dinsmore, a recent Irish immigrant, and John Neilson, also Irish, whom Jefferson described as "house joiners of the first order." Other artisans provided expert brickmaking, masonry, glazing, plastering, and

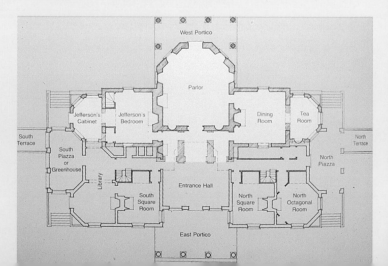

painting. John Holmes was the only workman to perish, when he fell from a scaffold in 1801.

> *"Architecture is my delight, and putting up and pulling down, one of my favorite amusements."*
>
> THOMAS JEFFERSON

During the winter of 1798, family members lived in the Parlor and Study as the roof of the original house around them was removed. Although Jefferson wanted the new roof put up right away, work was delayed, and it was finally finished, except for the dome, in April 1799. In 1800 the dome, the first on an American house, was erected.

As Jefferson managed the government from the nearly finished President's House (now called the White House), he continued to direct Monticello's construction, but not without difficulty. For example, two of the four stone columns on the east front were put up incorrectly in his absence and had to be taken down and re-erected.

By 1804 Jefferson's Bed Chamber, Cabinet, Book Room, Dining Room, and Tea Room were nearly finished, and workmen installed the weights and pulleys of the Great Clock in the Entrance Hall. Exterior blinds with both fixed and movable slats, glass for skylights, flooring plank, window sashes and doors, and a single piece of hand-blown glass for the Dome Room oculus were ordered from suppliers in Philadelphia, Washington, Richmond, and Boston.

In 1807, the southwest portico pediment was temporarily supported by the stems of four tulip trees. As Jefferson prepared to leave office in 1808, the Entrance Hall floor was painted green and the Chinese railing on the top of the house was finished and painted. Two louvered verandas, or porticles, were built flanking the greenhouse, and a bell system to summon slaves was installed. ■

Opposite: The first Monticello is highlighted. Above: The Great Clock was made by Peter Spruck in Philadelphia in 1792-1793.

Retirement

At last free from public service, Jefferson retired to Monticello in March 1809. The house was largely completed. He was joined by his daughter, Martha Jefferson Randolph, her husband Thomas Mann Randolph, and their large family, which would soon include eleven children. His younger daughter, Maria Eppes, had died in 1804.

At the age of sixty-six, Jefferson turned his creative energy toward the completion of a new octagonal dwelling at Poplar Forest, his plantation in Bedford County, Virginia, about eighty miles from Charlottesville. Jefferson retreated to the quiet of Poplar Forest, often with a granddaughter or two, for several weeks each year to inspect his farm and enjoy a quiet respite from the activity of Monticello.

Near the end of his life Jefferson founded the University of Virginia, chartered in 1819. He ded-

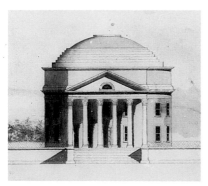

The Rotunda of the University of Virginia. Drawing attributed to John Neilson, February 1823.

icated himself to "this institution of my native state, the
hobby of my old age, … based on the illimitable freedom
of the human mind to explore." Jefferson helped select the
University's distinguished international faculty, chose books
for its library, and designed what he called "an academical
village," which is one of America's most celebrated architectural achievements.

Monticello after Jefferson's Death

Thomas Jefferson died on July 4, 1826, exactly fifty
years after the adoption of the Declaration of Independence. The national financial collapse of 1819 and other
factors had caused economic ruin for Jefferson. He died in
debt, owing over $100,000 to creditors. His heirs were
forced to sell his belongings, including his slaves, at an
auction held at Monticello in January 1827. In 1830 the
house and some of the land were sold to James Barclay,
who briefly attempted to establish a silk farm. After
Barclay's effort failed, Monticello was sold in 1834 to
Uriah Phillips Levy (1792-1862), a Jewish naval officer
who devoted himself to its preservation.

The Public Monticello

Jefferson received visitors and family members in Monticello's public rooms—the Entrance Hall, Parlor, Dining Room, and Tea Room.

The Entrance Hall

Jefferson regarded the double-storied Entrance Hall as a museum—one of the first in the country—where he could educate his family and visitors. Guests were intrigued by the "strange furniture of the walls"—maps, antlers, sculpture, paintings, Native American artifacts, and minerals.

The walls were hung with two Native American maps, drawn on leather, and eight or more large wall maps mounted on rollers, including one of Virginia as surveyed by Jefferson's father, Peter Jefferson, and Joshua Fry. To illustrate the natural history of North America, Jefferson displayed the antlers and horns of elk, moose, deer, American Big Horn sheep, musk ox, buffalo, and other animals.

Opposite: Entrance Hall. Below: Plan of the first floor of the remodeled Monticello.

1. Entrance Hall
2. Family Sitting Room
3. Book Room
4. Greenhouse
5. Cabinet
6. Jefferson's Bed Chamber
7. Parlor
8. Dining Room
9. Tea Room
10. North Piazza
11. Madison's Room
12. Correia's Room

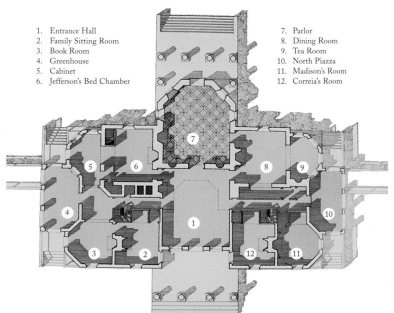

Among Jefferson's most prized specimens were the thigh, jawbone, and tusk of a mastodon found at Big Bone Lick, Kentucky.

The museum also contained at least forty Native American artifacts collected by Meriwether Lewis and William Clark on their famous expedition to the Northwest, which Jefferson had sponsored as President. Jefferson, with his longstanding interest in Native

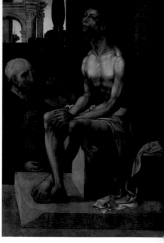

Jesus in the Praetorium, *copy after original by Jan Gossaert, 1527.*

Americans, wrote Lewis that he was "in fact preparing a kind of Indian hall." The most spectacular of the objects was a painted Mandan buffalo robe describing a battle scene. The pipes, clothing, and domestic objects that survive from Jefferson's collection are in the Peabody Museum

Martha Wayles Jefferson

Thomas Jefferson married Martha Wayles Skelton (1748?-1782) on New Year's Day 1772. When they met in 1770, she was the twenty-three year old widow of Bathurst Skelton and the mother of a young son. Her father, John Wayles, owned a plantation called The Forest in Charles City County, Virginia.

Too little is known about Mrs. Jefferson; no portraits of her survive. Family accounts describe her as small and attractive. She played the harpsichord and pianoforte, sharing a love of music with Jefferson, a violinist. Her surviving account books show that she kept careful records of the household economy.

Like many women of her day, Mrs.

"A single event wiped away all my plans and left me a blank which I had not the spirits to fill up."

THOMAS JEFFERSON
TO THE MARQUIS DE
CHASTELLUX, 1782

of Archaeology and Ethnology at Harvard University.

Eleven copies of Old Master paintings were hung on the walls. Of these, only two survive, *Jesus in the Praetorium* and *St. Jerome in Meditation.* Carved brackets, flanking the windows, supported busts of Voltaire, Turgot, and Alexander Hamilton. A colossal bust of Jefferson himself by Ceracchi was displayed on a green marble column, both now destroyed.

The Great Clock, made to Jefferson's specifications in Philadelphia in 1793, still dominates the Entrance Hall. Cannonball-like weights drive the dual-faced, seven-day calendar clock. The weights proceed down the south wall, passing by marks indicating the days of the week and traveling through a hole in the floor to reach the marks for Friday and Saturday. A Chinese gong on the roof strikes the hour; the hours are visible on the second face of the clock on the east portico.

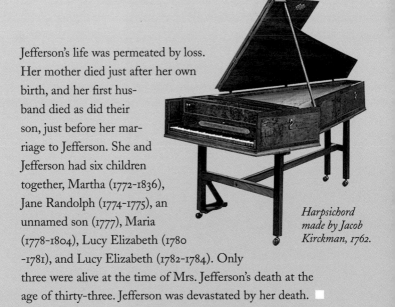

Jefferson's life was permeated by loss. Her mother died just after her own birth, and her first husband died as did their son, just before her marriage to Jefferson. She and Jefferson had six children together, Martha (1772-1836), Jane Randolph (1774-1775), an unnamed son (1777), Maria (1778-1804), Lucy Elizabeth (1780 -1781), and Lucy Elizabeth (1782-1784). Only three were alive at the time of Mrs. Jefferson's death at the age of thirty-three. Jefferson was devastated by her death. ▪

Harpsichord made by Jacob Kirckman, 1762.

The Parlor

The Parlor was the principal social space where the family gathered and invited guests to join them as they read, made music, played games, or took tea. Weddings and christenings were held in this room with its crimson draperies, eclectic tables, and seating furniture made in England, France, Philadelphia, and at Monticello. In his earlier years Jefferson played the violin, calling music "the favorite passion of my soul." Chairs were sometimes arranged in a circle when the Randolph children read together. Jefferson's favorite place for reclining was in a "campeachy" chair where his granddaughter Ellen recalled, "in the shady twilight, I was wont to see him resting."

The Parlor offered Jefferson an opportunity to educate his family and guests. He understood that the future of the United States depended upon the ability of its people to make informed decisions. Wanting, as he said, to "improve the taste of his countrymen," Jefferson exhibited fifty-seven works of art here. The walls were crowded with thirty-five portraits of men who had shaped Jefferson's values as well as American and world history. Most important were "the three greatest men that have ever

> "In the half hour that passed before candles came in as we all sat round the fire, he taught us several childish games, and would play them with us."
>
> A JEFFERSON GRANDDAUGHTER

Opposite: The Parlor. Above: Cittern given to granddaughter by Jefferson in 1816. Overleaf: The south wall of the Parlor.

lived"—John Locke, Isaac Newton, and Francis Bacon. (Only Locke's portrait survives, shown left.) Observing that "our country should not be without portraits of its discoverers," Jefferson obtained likenesses of Columbus, Magellan, Cortez, Raleigh, and Vespucci.

Jefferson's absent friends were represented in oil paintings and engravings—Washington, Franklin, Adams, Madison, Lafayette, David Rittenhouse, Thomas Paine, and others. The Parlor also featured eighteen copies of biblical, classical, and historical paintings, including a copy of Guido Reni's *Herodias Bearing the Head of Saint John.*

The Dining Room

The Dining Room received family members and guests for two meals each day, breakfast and dinner. While waiting for his family to gather, Jefferson often sat reading in one of a pair of small French armchairs; one of them is

the last chair Jefferson sat in before his death. A visitor noted "on the mantel-piece … were many books of all kinds." Another praised the behavior of Jefferson's grandchildren who "are in such excellent order, that you would not know, if you did not see them, that a child was present."

Because the Dining Room was located on the cold north side of the house, a window with triple-hung

Opposite: Dining Room. Above: Mantel showing dumbwaiter for wine.

sash was double-glazed to conserve heat. Two dumbwaiters, installed on either side of the fireplace, carried bottles of wine from the wine cellar below. A revolving serving door on a center pivot contained shelves for platters of food.

Rather than use a single dining table, Jefferson owned several that could be put together. When not in use, the tables were placed against the walls. The tables were decorated with French biscuit figurines and a glass épergne, a decorative serving piece. Various groups of chairs were used, including two different sets of mahogany shield-backs.

Above: Jefferson cup made by John Letelier, 1810. Left: Silver askos made by Simmons and Alexander, 1801.

Jefferson himself designed a pair of silver goblets as well as the familiar "Jefferson cups," tumblers made of silver given to him by George Wythe. A silver askos, a kind of Roman pouring vessel, was called the "duck" and used as a serving pot for hot chocolate.

The Tea Room

Separated from the Dining Room by double sets of pocket doors is the room Jefferson called his "most honorable suite." It contained an outstanding collection of portraits and provided another place where Jefferson could read and write. Thirty-four engravings, miniatures, and medals, mainly of American Revolutionary figures, ornamented the polygonal room. Plaster busts of Franklin, John Paul Jones, Lafayette, and Washington by the French sculptor Jean-Antoine Houdon were placed on console brackets.

Overleaf: Tea Room

Martha Jefferson Randolph

Jefferson's oldest daughter was born at Monticello on September 27, 1772. Ten years old at her mother's death, she shared her father's grief, establishing an affectionate bond that lasted throughout their lives. After her father's retirement from public service, Mrs. Randolph and her large family lived at Monticello, where she managed the household activities.

Young Martha accompanied her father to Paris in 1784 and was enrolled at a convent school. There she continued her study of literature, drawing, and music. She later lamented that she was ill-prepared for household management.

Soon after the Jeffersons' return from France in 1789, Martha married Thomas Mann Randolph, Jr., the son of Jefferson's old friend and later a governor of Virginia. Mrs. Randolph gave birth to twelve children, eleven of whom lived to adulthood. The children were Anne Cary Randolph Bankhead (1791-1826), Thomas Jefferson Randolph (1792-1875), Ellen Wayles Randolph (1794-1795), Ellen Wayles Randolph Coolidge (1796-1876), Cornelia Jefferson Randolph (1799-1871), Virginia Jefferson Randolph Trist (1801-1882), Mary Jefferson Randolph (1803-1876), James Madison Randolph (1806-1834), Benjamin Franklin Randolph (1808-1871), Meriwether Lewis Randolph (1810-1837), Septimia Anne Randolph Meikleham (1814-1887), and George Wythe Randolph (1818-1867). Mrs. Randolph died in Charlottesville in 1836. ∎

Martha Jefferson Randolph by James Westhall Ford, 1823.

The furniture in the Tea Room provided space for dining as well as for reading and writing. The oval mahogany table at the center of the room is identical to the one made at Monticello perhaps by John Hemings, the expert slave cabinetmaker. After his retirement Jefferson kept a comb-backed Windsor chair with a writing arm and a sofa or

Windsor couch here so that he could write with his legs outstretched. An inventory made after Jefferson's death lists a card table, two sofas, and nine mahogany chairs.

Above: Seau crénelé, Sèvres, 1787. Opposite: Dumbwaiter made by John Hemings in the Tea Room.

Maria Jefferson Eppes

Mary or Maria Jefferson Eppes (1778-1804), called Polly as a child, was Jefferson's second daughter. By all accounts she had "exquisite beauty." Abigail Adams remarked that she was the "favorite of every creature" in her house.

After her mother's death, Mary and her younger sister Lucy lived with their aunt Elizabeth Wayles Eppes and her husband Francis Eppes at Eppington in Southside Virginia. While Jefferson was in France, Lucy and a cousin died of whooping cough but Polly "got early over it." In spite of the emotional difficulty it posed, Jefferson determined that nine-year-old Polly would join him in Paris. Like her sister, she attended the Abbaye de Panthemont, studying French, music, and drawing, but she was never inclined toward her studies.

At Monticello in 1797, Maria married her childhood friend John Wayles Eppes (1773-1823), who later served in Congress. Mrs. Eppes gave birth to three children, dying after the complications of childbirth. Only her son Francis (1801-1881) lived beyond infancy. ▪

The Private Monticello

Mr. Madison's Room

Many friends and family visited Monticello, often for extended stays. Among the most frequent visitors were James Madison and his wife Dolley. Madison served as Secretary of State under Jefferson, who wrote of him, "There is no sounder judgment than his." This chamber was named for these special friends of the family.

The Madison Room is decorated with a reproduction of the colorful trellis wallpaper purchased for Jefferson in Paris in 1790.

Above: James Madison engraved by David Edwin after Gilbert Stuart, 1809. Below: Mr. Madison's Room.

Abbé Correia's Room

The Abbé José Correia da Serra (1750–1823), a Portuguese botanist, man of letters, and co-founder of the Academy of Science in Lisbon, visited Monticello seven times between 1812 and 1820, while he was Portugal's Minister Plenipotentiary to the United States. Jefferson called him "the best digest of science in books, men, and things that I have ever met with" and invited him to live at Monticello. He was such a popular visitor that the North Square Room, which served as a guest bed chamber, was named for him. A life portrait of the Abbé by Rembrandt Peale hangs above the mantel.

Above: Abbé Correia's Room. Right: Abbé Correia da Serra by Rembrandt Peale, c. 1812.

Family Sitting Room

After Jefferson's retirement, the family of Martha, his surviving daughter, and her husband, Thomas Mann Randolph, joined him at Monticello. The South Square Room became the Randolph family's principal private space. Martha Randolph also used the room as a school for her children and an "office" where she directed the work of the dozen slaves who worked as household servants in 1810.

As the Randolph daughters grew, Mrs. Randolph taught them the essentials of housewifery, including sewing. Among the contents of the room was a sewing table, made in the Monticello joinery, which stored prized needles, thimbles, and scissors. Mrs.  Randolph noted in her 1826 inventory that the room contained "7 old Mahogany chairs given by Mr. Wythe."

Opposite: Family Sitting Room. Above: One of seven Virginia-made side chairs given to Jefferson by George Wythe.

Jefferson's "Sanctum Sanctorum"

Jefferson's comfortable private quarters consisted of four connected rooms: his Bed Chamber, Cabinet, Greenhouse, and Book Room. These rooms were rarely entered by others.

Jefferson's Bed Chamber

Jefferson's habit was to arise at dawn, "as soon as he can see the hands of his clock, which is directly opposite his bed," Daniel Webster reported in 1824, and examine "the thermometer immediately, as he keeps a regular meteorological diary." The black marble obelisk clock he designed and had made in Paris still sits on a wall shelf at the foot of his bed.

Obelisk clock made by Chantrot, 1790.

The double-height bed chamber features an unusual double-sided bed alcove which connects with the Cabinet. The Cabinet side, however, could be closed off by a folding screen. A gilded mirror, hung opposite the triple sash window, reflected the daylight.

A crimson silk counterpane, sewn to Jefferson's specifications in 1808, covered his bed. His out-of-season clothing and extra bedcovers were stored in a closet, reached by a ladder, over the bed alcove. Garments for everyday wear hung on a "turning machine" with forty-eight arms placed at the foot of his bed.

"[Jefferson] asked us into what I had called his sanctum sanctorum, *into which it is very seldom any one is admitted."*

Margaret Bayard Smith, 1809

Opposite: Jefferson's "Sanctum Sanctorum," looking from the Book Room to the Cabinet. Overleaf: Jefferson's Cabinet (foreground) and Bed Chamber.

Thomas Jefferson by Rembrandt Peale, 1800.

On July 4, 1826, the fiftieth anniversary of the day that Congress approved the Declaration of Independence, Jefferson died in his bed at almost one o'clock in the afternoon. John Adams died later that same day, believing that Jefferson still survived.

The Cabinet

Jefferson spent much of the morning and late afternoon reading and answering correspondence in his Cabinet, or study. For convenience and comfort, he assembled a reading and writing arrangement in the center of the room that included a revolving chair, a writing table with a rotating top, a Windsor couch for resting his legs, and a revolving bookstand that could hold five open volumes at a time. Atop the writing table was a copying machine called a "polygraph," which duplicated Jefferson's letters as he wrote. At an architect's table brought from France, Jefferson designed the Rotunda, ten pavilions, and ranges of the "academical village" of the University of Virginia.

The contents of the Cabinet reflected Jefferson's interests and activities. His voluminous correspondence was stored in five filing presses and additional wooden cartons. "My own attachment to the exact sciences has made them the principal enjoyment of my leisure hours," he wrote in 1812. Scientific instruments in profusion— telescopes, microscopes, compasses,

Above: Jefferson's copying machine made by Peale and Hawkins, 1806. Opposite: Jefferson's Cabinet.

thermometers, an orrery, theodolite, circumferenter, and micrometer—indicated his "ardent desire to see knowledge disseminated through the mass of mankind." A tall case astronomical clock helped him calculate solar and lunar eclipses.

The Book Room

One of Jefferson's granddaughters wrote that "Books were at all times his chosen companions ... I saw him more frequently with a volume of the classics in his hand than with any other book."

Jefferson's library was among the largest in the country. After the British burned part of the Capitol in 1814, ravaging its book collection, Jefferson offered to sell his library to Congress for whatever price it was willing to pay. Jefferson's collection of about 6,700 volumes, acquired for $23,950, became the nucleus of the present Library of Congress. After the sale, Jefferson assembled a smaller retirement library of approximately 1,000 titles, including poetry, philosophy, and politics.

The books were stored in five different sizes of open wooden boxes with a shelf in the middle. They were stacked by size, with folios on the bottom, followed by quartos, octavos, duodecimos, and petit-format books at the top.

"From sun-rise to one or two o'clock, and often from dinner to dark, I am drudging at the writing table."

THOMAS JEFFERSON, 1817

The tall reading or architect's desk, made in Virginia, was large enough to support a folio. The octagonal filing table was particularly prized by the family.

The Book Room viewed from Jefferson's Cabinet.

The Greenhouse

A passionate gardener, Jefferson kept flowers, plants, and flats for sprouting seeds in the Greenhouse in his private quarters. Visitors commented that "the view of the plants it contains, is unobstructed" and that "the doors of the library opened upon both its beauty and fragrance."

Jefferson also may have kept a chest of tools and workbench here. He was capable of repairing his scientific instruments and carrying out "any little scheme of the moment in the way of furniture or experiment," a granddaughter noted. Isaac Jefferson, a slave, remarked that Jefferson was "as neat a hand as ever you see to make keys and locks and small chains, iron and brass. He kept all kind of blacksmith and carpenter tools in a great case with shelves to it."

"It is neither wealth nor splendor, but tranquility and occupation which give happiness."

THOMAS JEFFERSON

THE SECOND AND THIRD FLOORS

Narrow, steep stairways at both ends of the first floor passages reach the second and third floors, not currently accessible to visitors for safety reasons. In Jefferson's day, these floors were mainly occupied by the Randolph family, visiting family, and house guests. On the second floor, six rooms opened onto the north and south passages and were heated by iron stoves. Four bedrooms echoed the plan of the rooms below, with two square rooms and two rooms with semioctagonal bows. A rectangular fifth room, above the South Piazza, was used for extra sleeping space, storage, and a nursery. The sixth and smallest of the

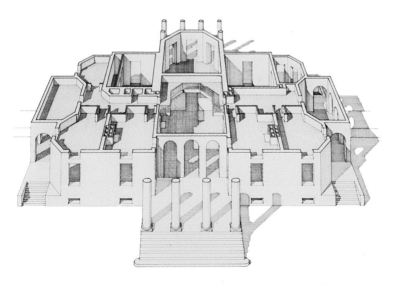

Above: Plan of the second floor. Opposite: Stairway to the third floor.

55

rooms, directly above the Cabinet, was called the
"Appendix" by the family, and probably provided extra
sleeping space.

The third floor contained what Jefferson called the
"Dome" or "Sky" Room and three unheated bedrooms.
A rectangular bedroom on the north side featured two bed
alcoves and two skylights. Each of the other bedrooms
had a skylight and one bed alcove.

The Dome Room

In spite of the Dome Room's beauty, a visitor reported
that it "was abandoned to miscellaneous purposes" because
of its inconvenience; the narrow stairs made it hard to
reach. Crowned by an oculus of handblown glass, the room

The Levy Family

Monticello's survival is the result of a pioneering preservation effort by Uriah Phillips Levy (1792-1862) and his nephew, Jefferson Monroe Levy (1852-1924). Born in Philadelphia, Uriah was the third of fourteen children of Rachel and Michael Levy, Jews of Portuguese descent. At the age of ten, Uriah ran away to sea, later enlisting in the United States Navy where he fought against flogging and defended religious freedom. Levy, an ardent admirer of Jefferson, commissioned the first public portrait of his hero in 1832.

Levy purchased Monticello for $2,700 in 1834. He dedicated himself to the protection of Monticello, writing that the houses of great men

Uriah Phillips Levy (1792-1862).

should be preserved as "monuments to their glory." His mother, Rachel Phillips Levy (1769-1839), was buried along Mulberry Row.

Levy died in 1862, bequeathing Monticello to the federal government, which relinquished its claim. Levy's heirs contested his will and lengthy litigation ensued. Uriah's nephew Jefferson Monroe Levy, later a congressman from New York, purchased Monticello in 1879. Monticello's condition had badly deteriorated, and Jefferson Monroe Levy committed himself to its restoration. He owned Monticello until it was acquired in 1923 by the newly formed Thomas Jefferson Memorial Foundation.

was painted Mars yellow. Jefferson's eldest grandson, Thomas Jefferson Randolph, and his bride Jane Hollins Nicholas lived there briefly after their marriage in 1815. Two granddaughters, Virginia and Cornelia Randolph, made a hideaway in the space above the portico, furnishing it with a sofa, tables, and chairs. After Jefferson's death, and possibly earlier, the Dome Room was used for storage.

The South Pavilion

Construction of the South Pavilion, believed to be the oldest brick building at Monticello, apparently began in the late spring or summer of 1770. Jefferson probably occupied it by November 1770. It was here that Jefferson brought his wife in January 1772; their first child, Martha, was born in

Below: South Pavilion in winter. Opposite: North Pavilion.

this building later that year. The Jeffersons lived in what he first termed the "outchamber" while the main house was under construction.

In 1808 Jefferson stored his law books in the South Pavilion, and by 1809, Charles Bankhead, a grandson-in-law, used it to study law. Later, the South Pavilion was sometimes used for parties, where, as a family member reported, "having procured a violin we danced until midnight." After 1824 Nicholas Philip Trist, a grandson-in-law and Jefferson's secretary, used the pavilion as a study.

The lower level of the South Pavilion functioned as Monticello's first kitchen until 1808, when the room was remodeled as a wash house, or laundry.

The North Pavilion

The excavation of the cellar of the North Pavilion began in 1802. Completed by 1809, the pavilion was used by Thomas Mann Randolph, Jr., Jefferson's son-in-law, as a study. On April 9, 1819, sparks from the chimney ignited the wood-shingle roof. The roof and probably the floor were destroyed but Jefferson noted "the walls remain good." Snow from the ice house prevented the spread of the fire to the terrace.

Jefferson intended to use the lower level room as a bathing room but his plan of "contriving a regular bath" was never implemented. Instead, by 1823, a large tub was built for that purpose, but it is not known where it was placed. After Jefferson's death this space was used as a wash house.

The Dependencies

The dependencies are located below the terraces and along an all-weather passageway in the basement of the main house. The Ware Room, Wine Cellar, and three other cellars were directly below the house, while the Kitchen, Cook's Room, Smokehouse, Dairy, and two other rooms for slaves were located below the south terrace. An ice house, stalls for horses, and space for carriages were situated below the north terrace.

Above: Aerial view of Monticello looking south. Below: The south terrace and dependencies.

The Kitchen

Completed in 1809, Monticello's existing kitchen replaced an earlier one in the basement of the South Pavilion. Outfitted with French copper cookware and up-to-date gadgets such as a macaroni machine and an ice cream freezer, it was among the best equipped kitchens in Virginia. One of its special features was a stew stove, a waist-high masonry platform with multiple burners—a precursor to a modern stove.

The Cook's Room

Located next to the kitchen, this room was occupied by the cook and the cook's family, who were all Jefferson's slaves. One of the first cooks was Ursula (1737-1800), purchased for Mrs. Jefferson because she was "a favorite housewoman," skilled in salting, curing, and smoking meats. In 1784, Jefferson brought James Hemings (1765-1801) with him to France, where he became an accomplished cook and pastry chef. After training his brother Peter (1770-1830+) to succeed him, he gained his freedom in 1796. Later cooks included Edith Fossett (1787-1857) and Fanny (b. 1788).

The Smokehouse

Although Jefferson preferred meat as a condiment, large quantities of meat were consumed at Monticello at breakfast and dinner. Beef, usually fresh, and pork, usually cured, were most common and were supplemented by mutton, lamb, veal, and rabbit. Pork was soaked and cured in the smokehouse.

The Ware Room

Locked like a vault with keys held by Mrs. Randolph and her daughters, the Ware Room contained Monticello's most valuable stores. Here were placed items imported from Richmond, Washington, and abroad—anchovies, almonds, pickles, sugar, chocolate, mustard, cheese, spices, olive oil, rice, beef tongues, and coffee.

The Wine Room

Jefferson cultivated a taste for wine while living in France. He visited notable vineyards in Bordeaux, Burgundy, and the Rhone Valley, including Château Latour and Château Haut-Brion. After he returned to

Lead glass wine glasses, c. 1800.

the United States, he imported wines from France, Germany, Hungary, Italy, and Portugal. Dumbwaiters lifted wine bottles directly from the Wine Room to the Dining Room above.

The Cellars

Three cellars were used for making and bottling beer and cider, as well as storing fat, hard soap, tallow, rum, and pipes of wine.

The Ice House

Ice was essential for the preservation of butter and fresh meat. It also, in Jefferson's view, promoted economy, "as it would require double the quantity of fresh meat in summer had we not ice to keep it." Every available wagon hauled ice from the Rivanna River to the newly constructed ice house in the winter of 1802-1803. It took "62. waggon loads of ice to fill it," Jefferson noted. In another year, 1815, the ice lasted until October 15.

THE
GARDENS OF
Monticello

Peter J. Hatch
Director of Gardens & Grounds

Thomas Jefferson's interest in gardening arose from a wide-eyed curiosity about the natural world. He chose the site for Monticello because of its sweeping prospects of the Piedmont Virginia countryside and intimacy with the busy "workhouse of nature." The landscape was his "workhouse" and the gardens at Monticello became an experimental laboratory. Jefferson approached natural history as a scientist; as an experimenter who aspired to observe and define seemingly all the natural phenomena "fabricated at our feet"—whether the wind direction, the blooming dates of wildflowers, or the life cycle of a destructive insect. But it was through gardening that he was able to participate in the motions of this physical world—grafting peach wood or sowing cabbages with his granddaughters. It was through horticulture that his experiments bore fruit, that his landscape assumed shape and form and color, that the drama of the natural world began to unfold under his personal direction.

GARDEN SCIENTIST

Jefferson was a zealous record-keeper. He has been described as the "father of weather observers" for his

Weather Memorandum Book, a detailed account of the daily temperatures, rainfall, and wind direction. One of his

most enduring legacies was his garden diary or Garden Book, edited by Edwin Morris Betts. This edition includes not only his personal garden diary, a "Kalendar" of plantings in his garden, short treatises on soil preparation for grape vines, and meticulous notes on how many "grey snaps" would fill a pint jar—but also extracts from the letters he wrote and received concerning gardening, natural history, and landscape design.

When Jefferson wrote, "The greatest service which can be rendered any country is to add a useful plant to its culture," he was expressing his hopes that the introduction of new economic plants could be a means of transforming American society. The staggering number of both useful and ornamental plants grown at Monticello, including 250 vegetable and 170 fruit varieties, attests to Jefferson's experimental approach. Monticello was a botanic garden of new and unusual introductions from around the world. The geographic homes of the plants grown at Monticello reflect the reach of his gardening interests: new species discovered by the Lewis and Clark expedition like the snowberry bush and flowering currant, Italian peach and grape

Above: Twinleaf, Jeffersonia diphylla. *Opposite above: "Kalendar" in the Garden Book for 1809. Opposite below: Vaga Loggia peach from Giorgio Gallesio,* Pomona Italiana, *1817.*

cultivars probably first grown in the New World by Jefferson himself, and giant cucumbers from Ohio over four feet long.

Botany, agriculture, even surveying were also essential components that formed the foundation for Jefferson's interest in both horticulture and landscape design. Monticello was the center of a 5,000-acre farm and Jefferson, at times, regarded himself first and foremost a farmer. An experienced draftsman and capable surveyor, invaluable technical aids for his ventures into landscape design, Jefferson was repeatedly measuring his roundabout roads or composing sketches of his estate. The woodland wildflower twinleaf, or *Jeffersonia diphylla,* was named in Jefferson's honor by the prominent Philadelphia botanist, Benjamin S. Barton, in 1792 at a meeting of the American Philosophical Society. Barton proclaimed that Jefferson's "knowledge of natural history … especially in botany and in zoology … is equalled by that of few persons in the United States."

"Humanized Horticulture"

For Jefferson, plants were intimately associated with people—friends, neighbors, political allies—and the exchange of seeds, bulbs, and fruit scions a token of enduring friendship. This union of gardening and sociability is evident throughout the letters in the Garden Book. Jefferson would chide his daughters and granddaughters for their inattention to the flower beds around the house, while they in turn would report on the latest horticultural dramas

Spring peas trained on "pea sticks."

taking place at Monticello. Jefferson also engaged in friendly competitions with his neighbors to determine who could bring the first English pea to the table in late Spring, the winner then hosting a community dinner that included a feast on the winning dish (or teaspoon) of peas.

Jefferson's essential philosophy of gardening was perhaps best summarized in a letter to his daughter Martha after she complained of insect-riddled plants in the Monticello vegetable garden: "We will try this winter to cover our garden with a heavy coating of manure. When earth is rich it bids defiance to droughts, yields in abundance, and of the best quality. I suspect that the insects which have harassed you have been encouraged by the feebleness of your plants; and that has been produced by the lean state of the soil." Such commitment to the regenerative powers of soil improvement suggests Jefferson's belief in the wholesome balance of nature and gardening. His response to the damage inflicted by the Hessian fly on his wheat crop revealed more a naturalist's curiosity about an insect's life cycle than a farmer's quest for a successful harvest. When Jefferson wrote that, for a gardener, "the failure of one thing is repaired by the success of another," he was expressing further this holistic approach to horticulture.

LANDSCAPE DESIGN

In a letter to his grand-daughter, Ellen, in 1805, Jefferson discussed the precise number of fine arts: "Many reckon but 5:

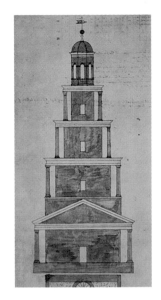

painting, sculpture, architecture, music & poetry. To these some have added Oratory … . Others again add Gardening as a 7th fine art. Not horticulture, but the art of embellishing grounds by fancy." Although his ideas on landscape evolved dramatically over his lifetime, Jefferson composed numerous fanciful schemes for the grounds of Monticello. He sketched over twenty designs for ornamental garden structures, some intended for the summit of Montalto ("high mountain"), which towers over Monticello ("little mountain") to the

Above: Jefferson's design for a structure (unbuilt) for Montalto. Below: Bean arbor at southwestern end of Vegetable Garden.

southwest. He also proposed a series of cascading waterfalls for Montalto and a romantic, classical grotto for the North Spring at Monticello. Most of these ambitious plans were never realized.

Jefferson toured English gardens in 1786 while serving as Minister to France. He wrote upon his return, "the gardening in that country is the article in which it surpasses all the earth, I mean their pleasure gardening." He was impressed by the newest landscape style in which garden designers attempted to imitate the picturesque schemes of eighteenth-century landscape painters and soften the distinctions between garden, park, and English countryside. This visit to England inspired many of Jefferson's ideas for the landscape at Monticello, including the planting of trees in clumps, the informal roundabout flower walk, and the Grove or ornamental forest. It also stimulated Jefferson's unifying vision for the grounds—the creation of an ornamental farm, or *ferme ornée*.

The Flower Gardens

Although there were earlier references to the flower "borders," it was not until 1807 that the flower gardens assumed their ultimate shape. Anticipating his retirement from the Presidency, Jefferson sketched a plan for twenty oval-shaped flower beds in the four corners or "angles" of the house. Each bed was planted with a different flower, most of which had been forwarded as seeds or bulbs from Bernard McMahon, the Philadelphia nurseryman and author of *The American Gardener's Calendar,* a favorite source of gardening information for Jefferson. The range of flower species planted in 1807 reflected the scope of Jefferson's interests: Old World florists' flowers, local wildflowers, plants of curiosity, the fruits of botanical exploration. In June of 1808 Jefferson sent his granddaughter, Anne, a plan for further plant-

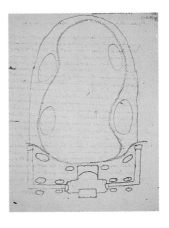

ings for the West Lawn: "I find that the limited number of our flower beds will too much restrain the variety of flowers in which we might wish to indulge, and therefore I have resumed an idea ... of a winding walk ... with a narrow border of flowers on each side. This would give abundant room for a great variety." The winding walk and the accompanying flower border were laid out in the spring of 1808, and by 1812, a need for a more systematic organization of the border required the division of the border into ten

Above: Jefferson sketch of West Lawn includes winding walk, flower border, shrubbery "clumps," and oval flower beds. Below: Winding walk with sweet william, larkspur, and lavender in early June.

"*The flowers come forth like the belles of the day, have their short reign of beauty and splendor, and retire like them to the more interesting office of reproducing their like.... the Irises are giving place to the Belladonnas, as these will to the Tuberoses etc. As your Mama has done to you, my dear Anne, as you will do ..., and as I shall soon and chearfully do to you all in wishing you a long, long, good night.*"

THOMAS JEFFERSON TO
ANNE CARY BANKHEAD, 1811

foot sections, each compartment numbered and planted with a different flower.

The flower gardens were cared for by Jefferson's daughters and granddaughters, often assisted by the slave gardener Wormley Hughes or by Jefferson himself, who would help with the design schemes, write labels, or set up a string line to assure straight rows. The flower gardens virtually

Winding walk with tulips in late April.

disappeared after Jefferson's death in 1826, but were restored by The Garden Club of Virginia between 1939 and 1941. Researchers found Jefferson's sketches of the beds and borders, and deciphered the depression of the winding flower walk by shining the headlights of their automobiles across the West Lawn at night. As well, perennial bulbs continued to flourish along the border 115 years after Jefferson's death, thereby outlining its location.

THE TREES OF MONTICELLO

Jefferson undoubtedly ranked trees at the top of his hierarchical chart of favorite garden plants. Visitors to Monticello were often given tours of the grounds which included a rambling survey of what one guest described as Jefferson's "pet trees." The image of lofty shade trees crowning the summit was consistently evoked by visitors to Monticello. Even in his most functional plantings Jefferson exploited the ornamental qualities of 160 species of trees. While serving as Minister to France between 1784 and 1789 Jefferson proudly distributed seeds of choice

North American trees to friends in Europe, continuing a tradition begun with the earliest European explorers in the New World. He has been described as "the father of American forestry" for an 1804 planting of white pine and hemlock. Thomas Jefferson's enthusiasm for the arboreal world was unrelenting. Two months before his death, at the age of 83, he designed an arboretum for the University of Virginia. He wrote, "Too old to plant trees for my own gratification I shall do it for posterity."

Several specimens, "original trees," have survived the inhospitable environment of mountaintop existence. These include a Red Cedar (*Juniperus virginiana*), a species which, surprisingly, Jefferson said was introduced into Albemarle County; the European Larch (*Larix decidua*), a deciduous conifer on the edge of the West Lawn; and two impressive Tulip Poplars *(Liriodendron tulipifera)* adjacent to the house. A Purple or Copper Beech *(Fagus sylvatica 'atropunicea'),* now growing in "an angle" of the west side of the house, is a replacement for an original tree blown down in the 1950s.

Grove in autumn.

THE GROVE

In 1806 Jefferson drew a sketch of Monticello mountain and designated eighteen acres on the northwestern side as the "grove." He envisioned a pleasure ground where "the canvas at large must be Grove, of the largest trees trimmed very high, so as to give it the appearance of open ground." Jefferson intended the Grove to be an ornamental forest with the undergrowth removed, the trees pruned and thinned, and the woodland "broken by clumps of thicket, as the open grounds of the English are broken by clumps of trees."

The Grove also included a planting of ornamental trees in an open area adjacent to the West Lawn. They were chosen for the contrasting textures of their foliage and included wild crab (*Malus coronaria*), chinaberry (*Melia azedarach*), umbrella magnolia (*Magnolia tripetala*), aspen (*Populus tremuloides*), and catalpa (*Catalpa bignon-*

ioides). In many ways, the lower or woodland part of the Grove represented Jefferson's ideal American landscape, where "gardens may be made without expense. We have only to cut out the superabundant plants." He said that "under the constant, beaming, almost vertical sun of Virginia, shade is our Elysium." Although it is uncertain how much of the Grove was actively maintained by Jefferson, a project was begun to recreate the concept in 1977. The existing forest was cleared and thinned; young trees, shrubs, and herbaceous flowers planted; and vistas, glades, and thickets introduced as Jefferson envisioned.

"I never before knew the full value of trees. My house is entirely embosomed in high plane-trees, and under them I break-fast, dine, write, read, and receive my company."

THOMAS JEFFERSON FROM PHILADELPHIA, 1793

THE VEGETABLE GARDEN

When Jefferson referred to his "garden," he, like most early Americans, was reserving the term for his 1,000-foot-long vegetable garden terrace on the southeastern side of his "little mountain." Although the garden served as a food source for the family table, it also functioned as a kind of laboratory where he experimented with seventy different species of vegetables. While Jefferson would grow as many as twenty bean varieties and fifteen types of English pea, his use of the scientific method selectively eliminated inferior sorts: "I am curious to select one or two of the best species or variety of every garden vegetable, and to reject all others from the garden to avoid the dangers of mixing or degeneracy." The garden evolved over many years, beginning in 1770 when crops were grown along the contours of

Below: Vegetable Garden and Garden Pavilion in summer. Opposite: 1812 Garden Book plan for organizing Vegetable Garden.

the slope. Terracing was introduced in 1806, and by 1812, gardening activity was at its peak. The terrace or garden plateau, literally hewed from the side of the mountain, was eventually described as a "hanging garden" by one visitor. The garden's dramatic setting is enhanced by the pavilion, used by Jefferson as a quiet retreat where he could read in the evening. It was reputedly blown down in a violent wind storm by the late 1820s, but was reconstructed in 1984 based on Jefferson's notes and archaeological excavations of its foundations.

The main part of the two-acre garden is divided into twenty-four "squares," or growing plots, and at least in 1812, the squares were arranged according to which part of the plant was being harvested—whether "fruits" (tomatoes, beans), "roots" (beets), or "leaves" (lettuce, cabbage). The site and situation of the garden enabled Jefferson to extend the growing season into the winter months and provided an amenable microclimate for tender vegetables such as the French artichoke. Because of favorable air drainage on a small mountaintop, late spring frosts are rare and the first freezing temperatures in the Fall rarely occur before Thanksgiving.

> *"No occupation is so delightful to me as the culture of the earth, and no culture comparable to that of the garden.... though an old man, I am but a young gardener."*
>
> THOMAS JEFFERSON, 1811

Much of the vegetable gardening itself seemed to have been delegated to the more elderly slaves, who were sometimes referred to as the "veteran aids." Jefferson's daughter,

Scarlet-runner beans.

Martha, in 1792, said the garden "does not bear close examination, the weeds having taken possession of much the greater part of it." However, Jefferson's meticulous notes on the day when peas were sowed or beans harvested suggests he was on-site, perhaps directing the work. Years after Jefferson's death, one of his slaves, Isaac, recalled, "For amusement he would work sometimes in the garden for half an hour at a time in right good earnest in the cool of the evening."

The recreation of the Monticello Vegetable Garden

If plants have sensibility...

Margaret Bayard Smith, a Washington friend, wrote to President Jefferson requesting a geranium plant that was growing in the windowed cabinet of the President's House (now the White House). She mentioned how the plant would be watered with her "tears of regret" at his retirement to Monticello. Jefferson responded in 1809:

"Rubens Peale with Geranium," by Rembrandt Peale, 1801.

began in 1979 with two years of archaeological excavations that attempted to confirm details of the documentary evidence. Archaeologists uncovered the remnants of the stone wall, exposed the foundation of the garden pavilion, and discovered evidence for the location of the entrance gate, which then ensured the squares were laid out according to Jefferson's specifications. While harvested vegetables are today distributed to Monticello employees, the garden also serves as a preservation seed bank of Jefferson and nineteenth-century vegetable varieties.

FRUIT GARDEN

Monticello's Fruit Garden, or "Fruitery" as Jefferson called it in 1814, sprawls below the Vegetable Garden and includes the 400-tree South Orchard; two small vineyards ("Northeast" and "Southwest"); berry squares of currants, gooseberries, and raspberries; a nursery where Jefferson propagated fruit trees and special garden plants; and "submural beds," where figs and strawberries were grown to take advantage of the warming microclimate created by the stone wall. On the other side of the mountain, Jefferson's

It is in very bad condition, having been neglected latterly, as not intended to be removed. He [Jefferson] cannot give it his parting blessing more effectually than by consigning it to the nourishing hand of Mrs. Smith. If plants have sensibility, as the analogy of their organisation with ours seems to indicate, it cannot but be proudly sensible of her fostering attentions. Of his regrets at parting with the society of Washington, a very sensible portion attaches itself to Mrs. Smith, whose friendship he has particularly valued. ■

North Orchard was reserved for cider apples and seedling peaches (peach trees grown from seed).

Both the Monticello Fruitery (including the South Orchard) and the North Orchard reflected the two distinct forms of fruit growing that emerged in eighteenth-century Virginia. The North Orchard was typical of the "field" or "Farm" orchards found on most middle-class farms: it was large, on average 200 trees, and consisted of only apple or peach trees. The fruit was harvested for cider, brandy, or as livestock feed. There is some truth to one historian's tongue-in-cheek remark that it was a significant event when Americans began eating their fruit rather than drinking it.

Royal George peaches in South Orchard.

On the other hand, the Monticello Fruitery resembled a gentleman's Fruit Garden in the Old World horticultural tradition, and was similar to the diverse recreational plantings of other wealthy Virginians such as George Washington. The trees, often planted with small fruits and even ornamentals, were grafted and included a wide spectrum of European varieties and unusual species like apricots and almonds, reserved, according to Jefferson, for the "precious refreshment" of their fancy fruit.

Nurseries

Jefferson had at least two nurseries: the "old nursery" below the garden wall and the terraced "new nursery," which was an extension of the northeast end of the Vegetable Garden. Here he propagated seeds and cuttings from friends and neighbors. The list of plants grown in the Monticello nurseries included his favorite species; he propagated thirteen kinds of shrubs, forty-one species of ornamental trees, twenty-six vegetable varieties, six kinds of grasses, eleven nut trees, and fifty-three fruit tree varieties in his nurseries. They were the heart of his pomological, if not horticultural, world. A nursery exhibit was recreated on the site of the "old nursery" in 1994.

"When he [Jefferson] walked in the garden and would call the children to go with him, and we were made perfectly happy by this permission to accompany him.... He would gather fruit for us,..."

VIRGINIA JEFFERSON TRIST, JEFFERSON'S GRANDDAUGHTER

FENCES

The Fruitery (as well as the Vegetable Garden) was enclosed with a variety of materials during Jefferson's fruit growing career: board fences, living hawthorn hedges, and even ditches that functioned as cattle guards. The most ambitious enclosure was the paling fence. Ten feet high, the fence extended nearly three quarters of a mile around the entire complex. The palings, or thin boards, were "so near as not to let even a young hare in." Although the paling gates were secured with a lock and key, overseer Edmund Bacon recalled fruit fights that arose when a band of schoolboys, rivals to Jefferson's grandson, Thomas Jefferson Randolph, broke down the palings and "did a great deal of damage" while pelting each other with unripe apples and peaches. A sample of the paling fence has been recreated along Mulberry Row.

THE SOUTH ORCHARD

Between 1769 and 1814 Jefferson planted as many as 1,031 fruit trees in his South Orchard. It was organized into a grid pattern in which he set out eighteen varieties of apple, thirty-eight of peach, fourteen cherry, twelve pear, twenty-seven plum, four nectarine, seven almond, six apricot, and a quince. The earliest plantings, before 1780, reflect the experimental orchard of a young man eager to import Mediterranean culture to Virginia and included olives, almonds, pomegranates, and figs. However, the mature plantings after 1810 included mostly species and varieties that either thrived through the hot, humid summers and cold, rainy winters of central Virginia, such as seedling peaches and Virginia cider apples, or else Jefferson's favorite fancy fruits like the Carnation cherry.

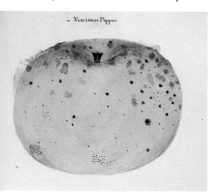

Newtown Pippin

The restoration of the South Orchard began in 1981 and was an attempt to recreate his mature, 1811 plan.

The peach might be regarded as Jefferson's favorite type of fruit tree: he planted as many as thirty-eight varieties, and in 1811 the South Orchard included 160 peach trees, far more than any other species. When Jefferson wrote his granddaughter in 1815 that "we abound in the luxury of peach," he was repeating a theme expressed by colonial fruit growers and even the first natural historians of the New World. Jefferson's favorite apples included Hewes's Crab, a cider apple widely distributed in colonial Virginia, and Taliaferro, "the best cyder apple existing." When comparing the fruits of Europe and America,

Jefferson wrote from Paris, "They have no apple to compare with our Newtown Pippin," which, with the Esopus Spitzenburg, were his favorite dessert apples.

VINEYARDS

Thomas Jefferson has been described as America's "first distinguished viticulturist," and "the greatest patron of wine and winegrowing that this country has yet had." Although he aspired to make a Monticello-grown wine, his continual replanting of the vineyards suggests a perennial and losing struggle with grape cultivation. But Jefferson was not alone. The successful cultivation in eastern North America of *Vitis vinifera,* the classic European wine species, was virtually impossible until the development of modern pesticides controlled such destructive pests as black rot and phylloxera, an aphid-like root louse. Many native grapes were more effectively grown, yet the poor

Black Hamburg grapes.

quality of the resultant wine impeded progress in the development of an established industry. The history of grape culture at Monticello suggests Jefferson's unrelenting oscillation between a desire to grow the difficult yet rewarding vinifera, and the possibilities of well-adapted New World alternatives—the fox grape (*Vitis labrusca*) and the Scuppernong variety of the southern muscadine (*V. rotundifolia*).

The two vineyards, Northeast (9,000 square feet) and Southwest (16,000 square feet), were ideally sited for grape growing in the heart of the South Orchard below the garden wall. The 1807 planting of 287 rooted vines and cuttings of twenty-four European grape varieties was the most ambitious of seven experiments. Jefferson's 1807 plan for the Northeast vineyard was restored in 1985; the Southwest vineyard was replanted in 1992. Jefferson's European varieties were grafted on the more resilient native rootstock to encourage hardiness and pest resistance. Because of a documentary suggestion that vines were "espaliered," a permanent structure based on an eighteenth-century American grape treatise was constructed.

The Thomas Jefferson Center for Historic Plants

The culmination of the restoration of Jefferson's gardens at Monticello was the opening of the Center for Historic Plants in 1987. The Center is an educational garden center devoted to the collection, preservation, and distribution of plants known in early American gardens. The Garden Shop, open from March to November, is located at the Monticello Shuttle Parking Area, where historic plants, heirloom seeds, and books on the history of garden plants are available.

Northeast vineyard with Garden Pavilion.

THE
Plantation

Lucia C. Stanton
Senior Research Historian

I n the years of his final retirement (1809-1826),
Jefferson left the house each midday to take his
daily exercise. After a walk down Mulberry Row to
inspect the workshops, he would mount his horse Eagle to
visit his farms and mills. Over a mile from the mountaintop he stopped at the Monticello farm quarters, where he
might discuss livestock with overseer Edmund Bacon.
Jefferson had four breeds of sheep and
was also improving his hogs by the
introduction of an African breed.

At the bottom of the mountain he
might observe activities at his sawmill
before fording the Rivanna River to
his Shadwell farm. There he had two
mills, one for grinding corn for home
use. The other, which Jefferson leased out, used the most
up-to-date milling machinery to process his and his neighbors' wheat crops. This "merchant mill" had its attendant
cooper's shops, where barrels were made for shipping the
flour down the river to Richmond.

Sometimes Jefferson would continue on to the small

> *"From breakfast to
> dinner, I am in my
> shops, my garden, or
> on horseback among
> my farms."*
>
> THOMAS JEFFERSON, 1810

town of Milton, three miles from his starting point. Here he might negotiate a contract for the sale of firewood from his surrounding woodlands or take his gun in pursuit of nearby quail. In his daily combination of exercise and plantation management, Jefferson might ride ten miles, never leaving his own property.

THE LAND

From his mountaintop Thomas Jefferson had a panoramic view of a plantation stretching almost four miles from one boundary to the other and bisected by the Rivanna River. By the purchase of additional land in the 1770s and 1780s, he had increased the 3,000-acre inheritance from his father to more than 5,000 acres.

Along with the land from his father, Jefferson had inherited a long-entrenched system of cultivation. Slave laborers, managed by overseers, raised crops of tobacco for

sale to a Scottish mercantile firm. This firm in turn sold Jefferson imported goods on credit. On the eve of the American Revolution, Jefferson, like many of his fellow Virginians, had by this practice accumulated a large debt to British merchants—£1,400 in his case.

"Agriculture, the employment of our first parents in Eden, the happiest we can follow, and the most important to our country."

THOMAS JEFFERSON, 1817

He had also acquired an abiding dislike for the culture of tobacco—"a culture," as he wrote in his *Notes on Virginia,* "productive of infinite wretchedness." He believed that tobacco impoverished the soil and that the laborious process of raising this staple crop diverted attention from other farm products essential to the health of the plantation's residents. Nevertheless, Jefferson continued to raise tobacco for thirty years.

On his retirement as Secretary of State in 1794,

Chimney of Joinery on Mulberry Row.

Who Lived at Monticello?

Thomas Jefferson and his family lived at Monticello with enslaved African Americans and free European and American craftsmen. The chart on the next four pages represents the population of this busy plantation in the late 1790s.

Thomas Jefferson
PLANTER
STATESMAN

Martha Jefferson
Randolph
JEFFERSON'S DAUGHTER

Thomas Mann
Randolph
PLANTER
MARTHA'S HUSBAND

Anne Cary
Randolph
CHILD

Maria Jefferson
Eppes
JEFFERSON'S
DAUGHTER

John Wayles Eppes
PLANTER
MARIA'S HUSBAND

Thomas Jefferson
Randolph
CHILD

Ellen Wayles
Randolph
CHILD

Cornelia Jefferson
Randolph
CHILD

Elizabeth Hemings
DOMESTIC SERVANT

Peter Hemings
COOK

James Hemings
COOK

Betty Brown
DOMESTIC
SERVANT

Melinda
CHILD

Edwin
CHILD

John Hemings
JOINER

Joseph Fossett
BLACKSMITH

Betsy
HOUSE
SERVANT

Wormley Hughes
GARDENER

Burwell Colbert
PAINTER
BUTLER

Brown
NAILMAKER

Robert Bailey
GARDENER

David Barnet
SAWYER

John H. Buck
MILLWRIGHT

Hugh Petit
OVERSEER

James McGee
CARPENTER

Jacob Silknitter
CHARCOALBURNER

William Davenport
CARPENTER

James Dinsmore
JOINER

Henry Duke
BRICKMASON

Reuben Perry
CARPENTER

William Page
OVERSEER

Richard
Richardson
BRICKMASON

David Watson
JOINER

Stephen Willis
BRICKMASON

Robert
CHILD

Nance Hemings
COOK
HOUSE SERVANT

Critta Hemings
HOUSE MAID

James
CHILD

Sally Hemings
LADY'S MAID

Beverly
CHILD

Jupiter
COACHMAN
STONECUTTER

Great George
OVERSEER

Ursula
DOMESTIC
SERVANT

George
BLACKSMITH

Isaac Jefferson
BLACKSMITH
TINSMITH

Iris
FARM
LABORER

Squire
CHILD

Joyce
CHILD

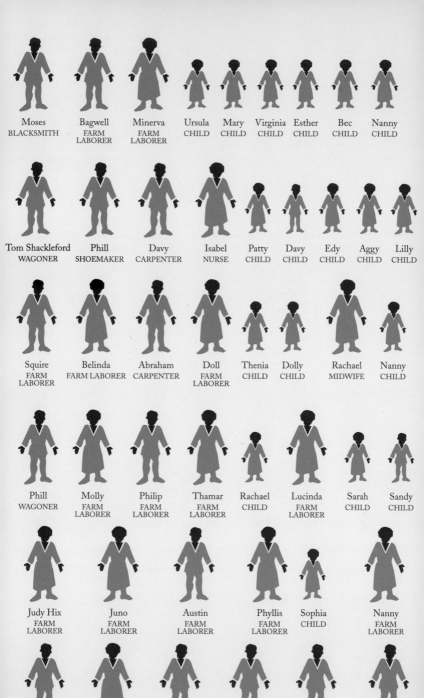

Moses
BLACKSMITH

Bagwell
FARM
LABORER

Minerva
FARM
LABORER

Ursula
CHILD

Mary
CHILD

Virginia
CHILD

Esther
CHILD

Bec
CHILD

Nanny
CHILD

Tom Shackleford
WAGONER

Phill
SHOEMAKER

Davy
CARPENTER

Isabel
NURSE

Patty
CHILD

Davy
CHILD

Edy
CHILD

Aggy
CHILD

Lilly
CHILD

Squire
FARM
LABORER

Belinda
FARM LABORER

Abraham
CARPENTER

Doll
FARM
LABORER

Thenia
CHILD

Dolly
CHILD

Rachael
MIDWIFE

Nanny
CHILD

Phill
WAGONER

Molly
FARM
LABORER

Philip
FARM
LABORER

Thamar
FARM
LABORER

Rachael
CHILD

Lucinda
FARM
LABORER

Sarah
CHILD

Sandy
CHILD

Judy Hix
FARM
LABORER

Juno
FARM
LABORER

Austin
FARM
LABORER

Phyllis
FARM
LABORER

Sophia
CHILD

Nanny
FARM
LABORER

John
GARDENER
CARPENTER

Amy
FARM
LABORER

Shepherd
NAILMAKER

Lewis
NAILMAKER

Barnaby
NAILMAKER

James Hubbard
NAILMAKER

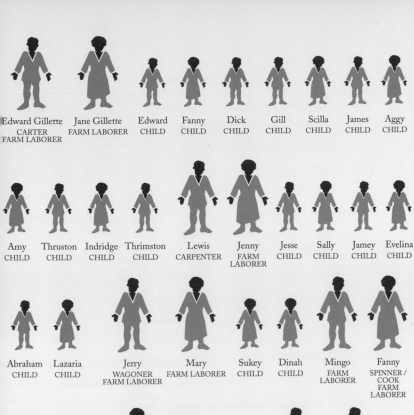

| **Edward Gillette**
CARTER
FARM LABORER | **Jane Gillette**
FARM LABORER | **Edward**
CHILD | **Fanny**
CHILD | **Dick**
CHILD | **Gill**
CHILD | **Scilla**
CHILD | **James**
CHILD | **Aggy**
CHILD |

| **Amy**
CHILD | **Thruston**
CHILD | **Indridge**
CHILD | **Thrimston**
CHILD | **Lewis**
CARPENTER | **Jenny**
FARM
LABORER | **Jesse**
CHILD | **Sally**
CHILD | **Jamey**
CHILD | **Evelina**
CHILD |

| **Abraham**
CHILD | **Lazaria**
CHILD | **Jerry**
WAGONER
FARM LABORER | **Mary**
FARM LABORER | **Sukey**
CHILD | **Dinah**
CHILD | **Mingo**
FARM
LABORER | **Fanny**
SPINNER /
COOK
FARM
LABORER |

| **Sousy**
CHILD | **Barrett**
CHILD | **Scilla**
FARM
LABORER | **Nelly**
CHILD | **Lotty**
CHILD | **Tim**
FARM
LABORER | **James**
FARM LABORER |

Sally
FARM
LABORER

Betty
FARM
LABORER

Caesar
FARM
LABORER

Toby
FARM
LABORER

Frank
CHARCOAL
BURNER

Goliah
FARM
LABORER

Phil Hubbard
NAILMAKER

Ben
NAILMAKER

Ben Hix
NAILMAKER

John
NAILMAKER

Davy
NAILMAKER

Bartlett
NAILMAKER

Jefferson finally began the long-planned reformation of his plantation. Describing himself as the "most ardent farmer" in Virginia, he initiated a new system of crop rotation that banished tobacco, included a soil-improving clover, and featured wheat as the staple crop. At the four farms that made up the Monticello

plantation, a total of 1,120 acres were cultivated in wheat, rye, Indian corn, red clover, potatoes, and field peas. Cattle and hogs foraged in the woods surrounding the fields and a small flock of sheep supplied Jefferson's table.

Jefferson actively sought to spread word of the latest agricultural improvements to his fellow countrymen. He was particularly zealous in the cause of soil conservation, championing crop rotation, contour plowing, and the use of gypsum plaster as a fertilizer. He experimented with new and improved crops and machinery and in this period devised his "moldboard of least resistance" for a plow. He hoped that the benefits of his portable horse-powered

threshing machines, based on a model he had imported from England, would be widely recognized.

After three years of retirement and intense daily involvement in the activities of his plantation, Jefferson was called back into public service as vice president. He was unable to continue the "system" he had inaugurated to reclaim fields that had been depleted by decades of the rotation of corn and tobacco. He was also discouraged by the difficulty of managing his enslaved farm laborers so that productivity was achieved without cruelty. "I am not fit to be a farmer with the kind of labour that we have," he wrote in 1799.

Although, in his later years, Jefferson turned most of his attention to the industries of his plantation, he never lost his progressive agricultural principles. He continued to advocate crop rotation and soil-improving crops, he tried to spread the benefits of improved breeds of sheep and hogs, and gave his support to new agricultural societies. Despite lifelong efforts to make his operations more efficient and productive, as well as imaginative enterprises, like a nailery and complex millworks, intended to provide additional financial support, Jefferson seldom made a profit from his

Jefferson's Moldboard

In the 1790s Jefferson developed his "moldboard of least resistance," an improved moldboard for a plow. Made on mathematical principles, it was intended to turn the cut sod over with the least expenditure of force and its systematic design allowed it to be easily duplicated. Jefferson's moldboard, which he used at Monticello, influenced some of the country's leading plow developers. He did not patent his invention, believing that he should not "monopolize by patent" any useful idea he might have.

plantation. His long career in public service prevented full attention to his personal affairs, while international wars and national crises affected the market price of his staple crops. Finally, severe agricultural depression after 1818 accelerated a deepening cycle of debt.

THE AFRICAN-AMERICAN COMMUNITY

In the 1790s, there were 120 enslaved men, women, and children living on the four farms that made up the Monticello plantation. Jefferson had inherited about 20 slaves from his father and acquired a further 135 slaves on the death of his father-in-law, John Wayles. The second largest slaveholder in Albemarle County in 1782, Jefferson owned for the rest of his life an enslaved population that

Above: 1816 cloth ration list of Monticello slaves by families. Below: Detail of Benjamin H. Latrobe's 1798 watercolor of a Virginia scene, "An overseer doing his duty."

numbered around 200—one-third of them living on his 5,000-acre Bedford County plantation, Poplar Forest.

Jefferson always believed that the institution of slavery was an "abominable crime." He was actively involved in ending the slave trade to Virginia in 1778 and, in the 1780s, in limiting the spread of slavery to the western territories. In his later years, however, he was criticized for taking no public leadership role in steps that would lead to the abolition of slavery. He privately advocated a plan of gradual emancipation that included the proviso that freed slaves be removed from the United States.

"My opinion has ever been that, until more can be done for them, we should endeavor, with those whom fortune has thrown on our hands, to feed and clothe them well, protect them from ill usage, [and] require such reasonable labor only as is performed voluntarily by freemen."

THOMAS JEFFERSON, 1814

In his *Notes on Virginia,* Jefferson expressed views on the natural inferiority of African Americans. Such opinions, at the root of his inability to envision a nation incorporating both black and white citizens, led him, like many other southerners of the Revolutionary generation, to adopt a paternalistic stance toward his own human property. Unlike George Washington, Jefferson did not free all his slaves, believing that giving freedom to "persons whose habits have been formed in slavery is like abandoning children." The seven enslaved men he did free were all artisans whose skills could be expected to earn them a measure of prosperity.

Jefferson often expressed concern for improving the living conditions of his own slaves. The food, clothing, and housing he provided, although inadequate by twentieth-century standards, were considered better than the southern standard. He also tried, with some success, to reduce the use of excessive physical punishment. Having, as he said, "scruples against selling slaves but for delinquency, or on their own request," Jefferson only reluctantly bought or sold slaves. Economic

Tin cup, probably made by Isaac Jefferson, found in Mulberry Row excavation.

difficulties, however, forced him to sell many slaves during his lifetime and his death left the remainder unprotected from sale and separation.

Monticello's enslaved laborers worked from dawn to dusk, six days a week. Besides those who raised crops or tended livestock, there were slave carters and wagoners, carpenters and blacksmiths, and spinners and weavers, as well as butlers, cooks, maids, and other domestic servants who worked in the house. The African-American families lived in log cabins along Mulberry Row and other roads

Personal possessions found in excavation of slave dwellings at Monticello.

near the mountaintop, or at the several farm quarters on the plantation. After 1808, some house servants lived in rooms in the south dependency wing of the house.

Jefferson's records indicate that a Monticello slave could expect to receive each week a peck of cornmeal, a pound of meat, some salted herring, and, occasionally, salt and milk. Each received a set of clothing every summer and winter, and a blanket every three years. Evidently no furnishings, except for certain cooking utensils, were provided for their cabins. It is apparent that Jefferson's slaves devoted much of their free time

Isaac Jefferson
(1775–c1850)

Daguerrotype of Isaac Jefferson, 1847.

The son of slave overseer Great George and
Ursula, a domestic servant, Isaac Jefferson was trained
as a metalworker. Thomas Jefferson took him to
Philadelphia to learn tinsmithing; he also worked in the
Mulberry Row nailery and was a skilled blacksmith.
Still practicing his blacksmithing trade as a free man at
age seventy-two, Isaac Jefferson left his recollections of
life at Monticello.

Peter Fossett, born at Monticello in 1815.

(at night and on Sundays and holidays) to supplementing these allotments. They worked in their gardens and poultry yards, raising extra vegetables and chickens to sell to their master; they fished and hunted to vary their diet; they made furniture and clothing for their own households and items like brooms and wooden pails to sell; they also performed tasks outside their working hours for which Jefferson paid them.

Nonetheless, all evidence suggests that, besides the

The Hemings Family

One of the remarkable enslaved families at Monticello was that of Elizabeth (Betty) Hemings (1735-1807). Jefferson inherited Betty Hemings and her children from his father-in-law, John Wayles. Over seventy of her descendants lived as slaves at Monticello, occupying some of the most important domestic and artisan's positions. Her daughters Bett (1759-1831+), Critta (1769-1850), and Sally (1773-1835) worked in the house, while Nance (1761-1827+) was a skilled weaver. Betty's son Robert (1762-1819) was Jefferson's personal servant and Martin (1755-1794+) was Monticello butler. James (1765-1801) and Peter (1770-1834+) were cooks, while Betty's youngest son, John Hemings (1776-1833), was a cabinetmaker and joiner.

Two of Betty Hemings' children lived some years in Paris while Jefferson served as U.S. minister to France. James Hemings had accompanied his master to Europe in order to learn the art of French cookery. His sister Sally came later, as personal attendant to Jefferson's younger daughter, Mary. Sally Hemings lived at Monticello, a domestic servant skilled in needlework, until Jefferson's death.

All seven slaves freed by Jefferson in his lifetime and in his will were Betty Hemings' sons or grandsons. Jefferson freed essential work, nights and Sundays in the slave quarters were also full of music and dancing, sports, religious observances, and the occasional midnight excursion in search of possum or wild honey. A number of Jefferson's slaves were eager to read and write, and they sought an education from their relatives or from members of Jefferson's family. As one former Monticello slave recalled, "I learned to read by inducing the white children to teach me the letters." Documentary records and oral history reveal strong family and community ties in the dwellings of Monticello's African Americans, where skills and values were passed from generation to generation.

Robert and James Hemings, at their own request, in the 1790s. His will bequeathed freedom to their brother John and four of their nephews: Joseph Fossett, Burwell Colbert, and Sally Hemings' sons Madison and Eston. Fossett (1780-1858) was head blacksmith at Monticello for many years; his wife Edith was head cook. Colbert (1783-1850+) was Jefferson's butler and personal servant after 1809. He was also a painter and glazier and later

French ointment jar found in excavation below Mulberry Row, possibly brought back from France by James or Sally Hemings.

worked at the University of Virginia. Madison (1805-1877) and Eston Hemings (1808-1856) learned the carpenter's trade from their uncle John and were also noted musicians. In 1873 Madison Hemings spoke about his life at Monticello and his belief that he and his siblings were the children of Thomas Jefferson. This connection was denied by Jefferson's family, and the issue has been part of American public discourse for two centuries. Because of genetic testing in 1998 and an ensuing review of other kinds of evidence, most historians today accept the truth of Madison Hemings's statement and believe that he and his siblings were Thomas Jefferson's children.

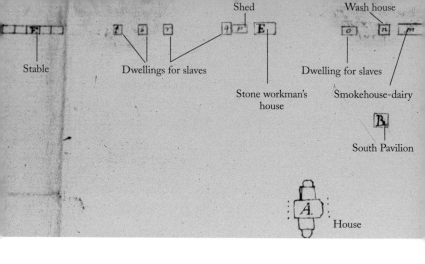

Stable

Dwellings for slaves

Shed

Stone workman's house

Dwelling for slaves

Smokehouse-dairy

Wash house

South Pavilion

House

MULBERRY ROW

The hub of plantation operations at Monticello was a 1,000-foot-long road Jefferson called Mulberry Row, after the trees that lined it. At the height of activity in 1796, there were seventeen structures along Mulberry Row, from the stable at its northeast end to the sheds for storing charcoal to the southwest. In between were five log dwellings for slaves, a stone house for free resident workmen, a wash house, a smokehouse and dairy, a blacksmith shop and nailery, two woodworking shops, and buildings for storage.

"To be independent for the comforts of life, we must fabricate them ourselves."

THOMAS JEFFERSON, 1816

Since most of these structures were built of wood, little survives from Jefferson's time. The stone workmen's house, altered over the years, today contains offices. Only portions of two other buildings remain—the stone stable, once home to Jefferson's saddle and carriage horses, and the stone chimney of the joinery, where much of the fine architectural woodwork for the house was crafted.

The long-vanished slave dwellings varied in size, from 12 to 14 feet wide and from 12 to 20 feet long. Built of hewn

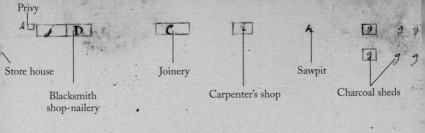

Privy
Store house
Blacksmith shop-nailery
D.
Joinery
Carpenter's shop
Sawpit
Charcoal sheds

Jefferson's diagram of Mulberry Row structures in 1796.

chestnut logs and roofed with pine slabs, they had log chimneys and earth floors.

With its woodworking and ironworking shops and its textile operations, Mulberry Row made Monticello a kind of industrial village, independent and self-sustaining. The enslaved artisans, often trained by hired white craftsmen, achieved a high level of expertise in a variety of trades. Because the building and remodeling of the main house required artisans of exceptional skill, both enslaved and free, Monticello exemplified far more than just the usual southern plantation self-sufficiency. Monticello's workmen eventually carried their craftsmanship well beyond the mountaintop, in the construction of the University of Virginia, and of dwellings, taverns, and courthouses elsewhere in the country.

Artist's recreation of Monticello and Mulberry Row in 1812.

Industry At Monticello

Wooden posts now mark the foundations of the combined blacksmith shop and nailery on Mulberry Row. Jefferson established the nailery in the 1790s to provide a new source of income while his farms were being brought back into production. Each day slave boys, aged ten to twenty, made 8,000 to 10,000 nails, which were sold to neighbors and local storekeepers. During his 1794-1796 retirement Jefferson monitored the daily performance of the young nailmakers, weighing the iron and nails to calculate their productivity and efficiency. Initially quite profitable, the nailery later suffered from indifferent management and an influx of cheaper imported nails.

The effects of the Embargo of 1807 and the War of 1812 on the supply of imported European goods impelled Virginians to turn more seriously to household manufacture, especially of cloth. In this period Jefferson expanded his textile production in order to provide the 2,000 yards of cloth he needed for Monticello's slave families. He also mechanized his operations, which may at one time have been located in the stone workmen's house on Mulberry Row. A carding machine prepared the raw fiber for the spinners, who operated Hargreaves spinning jennies of twenty-four and forty-eight spindles. Using looms with fly shuttles, the weavers turned the spun cotton, wool, and hemp into bolts of cloth. In 1815 there were thirteen women and children working in the textile shop.

Hargreaves spinning jenny.

Above: Chimney of Joinery. Below: Campeachy chair made by John Hemings.

Joinery

The woodworking shop on Mulberry Row was the site of the crafting of some of the finest architectural woodwork in Virginia. Hired white joiners like Irishmen James Dinsmore (c1771-1830) and John Neilson (c1775-1827) came to Monticello to work on the construction of the house and passed their skills on to slaves like John Hemings (1776-1833) and Lewis (c1758-1822). Hemings and Lewis also became skilled cabinetmakers, making chairs, tables, and desks. Hemings was freed by Jefferson in his will. ■

Unearthing History
at Monticello

Archaeological research plays an important role in the attempt to recover a more complete picture of the complex social and economic community that flourished at Monticello during Thomas Jefferson's lifetime. Monticello's archaeologists have investigated the below-ground traces of the plantation outbuildings that once stood along Mulberry Row and the orchards and Vegetable Garden to the south of it. During this work, thousands of artifacts were recovered, along with the remains of vanished buildings, fences, and other landscape features. Fitting these pieces of evidence together into a coherent historical narrative is an ongoing process.

By studying the stylistic motifs on the sherds of pottery recovered from them, archaeologists can infer when vanished buildings were used and monitor change in how people lived.

Houses constructed along Mulberry Row for enslaved workers in the 1770s had one or two large rooms. In the 1790s, houses with a single smaller room became the norm. This change was important to Mulberry Row's inhabitants because it meant they were less likely to share living space with unrelated individuals and more likely to live in smaller family groups.

Animal bones from the Mulberry Row sites also offer tantalizing clues about changing ways of life. The bones show that enslaved people living on Mulberry Row supplemented

Above: Items of personal adornment lost by individuals who lived on Mulberry Row: a wooden ring, silver Spanish coins pierced to be worn around the neck, and a cowrie shell from the Indian Ocean.

The excavated foundation of Building O on Mulberry Row which was occupied from 1770-1800, probably by members of two enslaved families.

the food provisions they received from Jefferson by hunting wild animals and that the frequency of this activity, and the implied mobility, increased from the late eighteenth to the early nineteenth century.

Both the shift to family housing and the greater importance of wild foods in the diet coincide in time with Jefferson's switch from tobacco cultivation to a more diversified agricultural regime centered around wheat. The new economic strategy required new crop mixes and rotations, increased reliance on fencing, plows, harrows, wagons, and mills, and more intensive animal husbandry for manure and plowing. Work regimes became more varied, complex, and less easily supervised. This may have offered slaves greater leverage in negotiating for marginal improvements in their lives.

Archaeological research at Monticello is reaching beyond the confines of the mountaintop. Archaeologists are conducting the first systematic archaeological survey of the 2,000 acres of land that formed the core of Jefferson's 5,000-acre plantation. The survey is designed to locate and document the remains of the vanished houses of Monticello's agricultural workers, along with the barns, mills, and roads that were the economic backbone of the plantation community.

—Fraser Neiman, Director of Archaeology

THE BURIAL GROUND

Thomas Jefferson is buried with other members of his family at Monticello in a burial ground chosen by himself in 1773. First laid out on the occasion of the death of his closest friend and brother-in-law, Dabney Carr, this plot is still owned by an association of Jefferson's descendants, and is still being used as a burial place.

Jefferson characteristically left precise instructions as to what should be inscribed on his tombstone:

the following inscription, & not a word more
'Here was buried
Thomas Jefferson
Author of the Declaration of American Independance*
of the Statute of Virginia for religious freedom
& Father of the University of Virginia.'
because by these testimonials that I have lived,
I wish most to be remembered.

In spite of his wishes, the dates of his birth and death were added to his tombstone, which is a replacement for the smaller obelisk that originally marked Jefferson's grave. His birthdate is given Old Style (O.S.) because he was born before the calendar reform of 1751, which advanced the calendar eleven days, causing his birthday to fall on April 13.

* Jefferson's own spelling.

A Thomas Jefferson Chronology

	PUBLIC	PRIVATE
1735		Peter Jefferson, Thomas Jefferson's father, patented 1,000-acre tract which became Monticello.
1743		Thomas Jefferson born at Shadwell.
1757		Peter Jefferson died.
1760-62		Thomas Jefferson attended the College of William and Mary.
1762		Began study of law with George Wythe.
1764		Came into inheritance at age 21.
1767		Admitted to practice of law before General Court.
1768	Elected to House of Burgesses.	Leveling of Monticello mountaintop begun.
1770		Construction begun. Shadwell burned. Moved to South Pavilion at Monticello.
1772		Married Martha Wayles Skelton. Daughter Martha born.
1773		Graveyard at Monticello established with the interment of Jefferson's friend and brother-in-law Dabney Carr.
1774	Wrote *A Summary View of the Rights of British America*.	Retired from legal practice. Inherited 11,000 acres of land and 135 slaves from his father-in-law. Laid off ground for kitchen garden. Daughter Jane Randolph born.
1775	Elected to Continental Congress.	Daughter Jane Randolph died.
1776	Drafted Declaration of Independence. Elected to Virginia House of Delegates. Appointed to revise Virginia laws.	Mother Jane Randolph Jefferson died.

Bust of Jefferson by Jean-Antoine Houdon, 1789.

A Thomas Jefferson Chronology

	PUBLIC	PRIVATE
1777	Drafted Virginia Statute for Religious Freedom, passed by General Assembly in 1786.	Unnamed son born and died.
1778	Drafted Bill for the More General Diffusion of Knowledge.	Daughter Mary (Maria) born. Brickwork of first house completed.
1779-81	Served as Governor of Virginia.	
1780		Daughter Lucy Elizabeth born. Began *Notes on the State of Virginia*.
1781		British troops at Monticello. Daughter Lucy Elizabeth died.
1782		Second Lucy Elizabeth born. Wife Martha died. First house substantially completed.
1783	Elected delegate to Congress.	
1784-89	In France as Commissioner and Minister.	
1784		Daughter Lucy Elizabeth died.
1787	Published *Notes on the State of Virginia*.	
1790-93	Served as first United States Secretary of State.	
1794		Began commercial manufacture of nails on Mulberry Row. Manumitted slave Robert Hemings.
1796		Remodeling and enlarging of Monticello begun. Manumitted slave James Hemings.
1797-1801	Served as United States Vice President.	
1797-1815	Served as president of the American Philosophical Society.	

A Thomas Jefferson Chronology

	PUBLIC	PRIVATE
1800		Dome constructed.
1801–09	Served as United States President.	
1803	Louisiana Purchase concluded. Lewis and Clark expedition launched.	
1804		Daughter Maria Jefferson Eppes died.
1806	Lewis and Clark expedition concluded.	House at Poplar Forest begun.
1807		Oval flower beds near house laid out. Shadwell merchant mill completed.
1808		North Pavilion completed and South Pavilion remodeled. Winding walk and flower beds on West Lawn laid out.
1809	Retired from presidency and public life.	Remodeling of house and construction of dependencies largely completed. Vegetable garden platform completed.
1812		Garden Pavilion constructed.
1815	Sold 6,700-volume library to Congress.	
1817	Cornerstone of Central College (later University of Virginia) laid.	
1822–25		House roof recovered with tin shingles.
1824		Historic reunion with the Marquis de Lafayette at Monticello.
1825	University of Virginia opened.	
1826		Died at Monticello, July 4.

A Declaration by the Representatives of the UNITED STA

F AMERICA, in General Congress assembled

When in the course of human events it becomes necessary for ~
solve the political bands which have connected them with another, and

~me among the powers of the earth the separate and equal ~~~~~~~~ state
which the laws of nature & of nature's god entitle them, a decent ~
the opinions of mankind requires that they should declare, the ca~
~hich impel them to the separation.

We hold these truths to be self-evident; that all m~
~eated equal & independent, that they are endowed by their creator w~
~~~~~~~~~~ inherent & inalienable, rights that among these are the ~~~~~~~
~fe & liberty, & the pursuit of happiness; that to secure these ~
~ernments are instituted among men, deriving their just power
~he consent of the governed, that whenever any form of governor
~ill becomes destructive of these ends, it is the right of the people
to abolish it, & to institute new government, laying it's founda~
~ts principles & organising it's powers in such form, a to 'her
~m most likely to effect their safety & happiness.   prudence ~
~ll ~~~~~ that governments long established should not be c~~~~~~
~pt & transient causes and accordingly all experience hath show
~ankind are more disposed to suffer while evils are sufferable tha
~pt themselves by abolishing the forms to which they are accustome
~or a long train of abuses & usurpations [begun at a distinguished]
~~~~~~~ invariably the same object, evinces a design to ~~~~~ ~
~~ ~~~~~~~~~ ~~~~, it is their right, it is their duty, to throw off
~~~~~~~ & to provide new guards for their future security. such
~~ the patient sufferance of these colonies; & such is now the necess
~ich constrains them to expunge their former systems of governm
~ history of the present king of great Britain is a history of unremitting injuries
~urpations [among which appears no solitary fact ~~~~~~~~~~~~~~~~~~ to co~
~t the uniform tenor of the rest [all of which have in direct object
~ablishment of an absolute tyranny over these states. to prove this let

JEFFERSON
AND THE
Living

Merrill D. Peterson
University of Virginia

A mong the American founders none made a larger contribution to what a wise philosopher, Alfred North Whitehead, once called "the symbolic code" of the nation than Thomas Jefferson. Americans would do well to take stock of that contribution and to reassess its meaning before the challenges of rapidly changing times. "The art of free society," according to Whitehead, "consists in the maintenance of the symbolic code; and secondly in fearlessness of revision, to secure that the code serves those purposes which satisfy an enlightened reason. Those societies which cannot combine reverence to their symbols with freedom of revision, must ultimately decay either from anarchy, or from the slow atrophy of a life stifled by useless shadows."

Thus it is that when we inquire into Jefferson's legacy to America and the world at the close of

Above: The "Edgehill" portrait of Thomas Jefferson by Gilbert Stuart, 1805. Opposite: Jefferson's "rough draft" of the Declaration of Independence.

Asher Durand's engraving of John Trumbull's Declaration of Independence.

the twentieth century we must look past the historically circumscribed elements of his life and thought to those principles and purposes that are timeless. As Woodrow Wilson remarked several generations ago, Jefferson's objects have not fallen out of date. "They are our objects, if we are faithful to any ideals whatever; and the question we ask ourselves is not, How would Jefferson have pursued them in his day? but How shall we pursue them in ours? It is the spirit, not the tenets of the man, by which he rules us from his urn."

No man's philosophy was more cordial to this spirit than Jefferson's. Although sometimes viewed as a doctrinaire, or as a guardian of tradition, Jefferson was actually a friend of innovation and change—an early champion of the idea of the progress of mankind. He believed, with other votaries of the Enlightenment, that the future would be better than the past and that light and liberty were on steady advance. As he told the doubting John Adams, "he steered his bark with hope in the head, leaving fear astern." In his philosophy the American Revolution was a revolt

not alone against Great Britain but against the past. In
1789, the year of the French Revolution, he set forth the
theory that "the earth belongs to the living generation."
Calculating from mortality tables the life of a generation
during its majority at just over nineteen years, he maintained that no public debt should be passed on to its successors
and that fundamental laws and constitutions should be
subject to review and revision at this term to ensure that
they did, indeed, continue to serve the purposes that
satisfied an enlightened reason. The theory could not readi-
ly be reduced to practice, but it entered into the spirit of
American democracy. In America, Alexis de Tocqueville
observed, "every man forgets his ancestors" and "each generation is a new people." Americans lived at the future, ever
on new frontiers, and they took nature rather than history
as their guide.

Much of Jefferson's world is lost today. He spoke of
the United States as "a chosen country, with room enough
for our descendants to the thousandth and thousandth generation." We live in the shadow of this vision. At its center
was the independent farmer, possessed of landed property,
and reared a sturdy citizen of the republic. The vision drove
the conquest of the continent and inspired Americans to
couple the mastery of nature with the pursuit of freedom
and happiness. The vision is archaic. The country is now
reckoning its costs in human and environmental devasta-
tion. Propertied independence is no longer an attainable
goal for most people; and we are compelled to replace the
old agrarian ethic with one that is responsible to the preservation of the natural environment. Jefferson, were he
among the living, would surely approve. In his famous gen-
erational theory he maintained that just as one generation

could not burden posterity with its debts so it could not "eat up the usufruct of the lands for several generations to come," for then "the lands would belong to the dead and not to the living."

Some of Jefferson's political and constitutional doctrines fall short of the standards of modern democracy and would, if firmly adhered to, defeat the liberal ends he had in view. His advocacy of the strict construction of the written constitution, for instance, has often been wielded as a weapon by conservative interests to hold back the exercise of governmental power for benign purposes. In fact, Jefferson never objected to novel uses of power to advance the public good; it was only that in his philosophy every exercise of power should be sanctioned by "the consent of the governed." If it was not authorized by the constitution it should be provided by amendment. He opposed his rival Alexander Hamilton's doctrine of "implied powers" and its later elaboration by Chief Justice John Marshall in the power of judicial review, whereby the United States Constitution was accommodated to the changing crises of affairs. Jefferson's approach to the problem proved impracticable. He acknowledged this implicitly during a crisis of his own presidency when he set aside his call for a constitutional amendment to sanction the Louisiana Purchase retroactively, thereby on his own admission making the Constitution "blank paper by construction." A constitution

Jefferson's revolving bookstand.

to remain vital ought to be continually renewed by the people. Jefferson knew, as he said, "that laws and institutions must go hand in hand with the progress of the human mind. As that becomes more developed, more enlightened, as new discoveries are made, new truths disclosed, and manners and opinions change with the change of circumstances, institutions must advance also, and keep pace with the time." And he offered the homely metaphor of a man forced to wear a coat that fitted him as a boy to illustrate the absurdity of regimenting a free and dynamic society under the forms of an old constitution.

Jefferson's openness to change is one of the most extraordinary things about him. To this there was one great exception. "Nothing is unchangeable," he wrote, "but the inherent and unalienable rights of man." The philosophy of human rights set forth in the Declaration of Independence became, more than the moral justification of that act, the creed of the new nation. Jefferson worked incessantly to advance the revolutionary promise of freedom, equality, and the pursuit of happiness. It is sometimes said that because he lived and died a slaveholder the creed was hollow. But there are times in history when words speak louder than incorrigible realities. Jefferson's words, in 1776, created their own monument. As Abraham Lincoln later said, Jefferson's "self-evident" truths became "the definitions and axioms of free society." To be sure, slavery stood in blatant contradiction to them. But Jefferson, with many of the founders, meant that the creed should be realized as fast as circumstances permitted. "They meant," Lincoln maintained, "to set up a standard maxim for free society, which would be familiar to all, and revered by all; constantly looked to, constantly labored for, and even though never perfectly

attained, constantly approximated, and thereby constantly spreading and deepening its influence, and augmenting the happiness and value of life to all people and of all colors everywhere."

To some of the most disturbing problems of American society today—poverty, violence, drugs, abortion—Jefferson's legacy offers no guidance. In certain areas, however, it is as clear and sure as it was in his own lifetime. His commitment to the twin principles of religious freedom and separation of church and state, for instance, may be more serviceable now than when the great Virginia Statute for Religious Freedom was enacted in 1786. An eloquent manifesto not alone of religious freedom but of intellectual freedom of the widest latitude, the statute was a mandate for government to keep hands off of religion and, of course, vice versa. The same principle found expression in the "free exercise" clause of the first Amendment. In the many public law cases that have invoked its protection over the last half-century it has sometimes been difficult for the Supreme Court to trace the boundaries of Jefferson's "wall

of separation between church and state." When, in recent years, the court became more tolerant of state intervention in the field of religion, Congress, fortunately, has pulled it back. The enactment of the Religious Freedom Restoration Act in November 1993 was a majestic affirmation of the continuing power of Jefferson's legacy. We are only now beginning to appreciate how far the principles that Jefferson believed would further peace and good will among a multitude of sects in America might also contribute to peace among religious and ethnic groups internationally.

Thomas Jefferson was a prophetic figure for American public education. As early as 1778, in Virginia, he proposed a complete system of public education from elementary schools through a state university. The fact that the proposal originated during a war for freedom and self-government was no accident; for Jefferson believed that the future of republican government depended upon an educated citizenry. As the people are "the only safe depositories of their own liberty," so they must be educated to a certain degree and prepared to take part in public affairs. Hence education became a paramount responsibility of government. From generation to generation the American democratic experience has vindicated the truth of Jefferson's vision. In our time, unhappily, confidence in that vision has been badly shaken, and the very idea of public education—of schools in the service of a civic ideal—is under attack. Renewal of the vision depends upon restoring the Jeffersonian nexus between education and democracy. It depends, in part, upon combatting the rampant cynicism toward American political institutions, from which even the young are not immune, and renewed commitment to the nation's fundamental values and goals together with keen understanding of the ways of pursuing them. President Clinton, once asked to what high position he would appoint Thomas Jefferson, should he return among us, responded unhesitatingly, "I would make him Secretary of Education." Nothing else, certainly, would present Jefferson with a late twentieth-century challenge more consonant with his eighteenth-century vision.

Jefferson remains the premier historical symbol of American freedom. It is a symbol too precious to lose among the lengthening shadows of the past. While parts of Jefferson's legacy, like religious freedom and public education, require little revision to serve present purposes, other parts must be separated from their historical baggage and reconstructed in the light of modern conditions. It is not by rote copying or parroting of Jefferson that his values and goals will be realized but by a keen sense of history joined to works of creative intelligence.

— 1994

Thomas Jefferson by Thomas Sully, 1821 (detail).

GREETINGS

from the President
of the
Thomas Jefferson Foundation

Every year we welcome over half a million visitors to
Monticello with the goal of providing an enjoyable experience and of helping people to think historically about
America's "architect of democracy." We hope this guidebook will contribute knowledge and insight about the
home of Thomas Jefferson, the man himself, and his legacy
across the centuries.

Monticello is owned and operated by the Thomas
Jefferson Foundation, a private, nonprofit corporation. Our
mission is straightforward: preservation and education. We
are committed to the aggressive stewardship of a finite
resource—Monticello, the only home in America on the
World Heritage List, which is a compilation of international treasures (including the Great Wall of China and the
pyramids of Egypt) that must be protected at all costs. We
are equally vigorous about wanting to share with broad
audiences what we learn about Thomas Jefferson.

Prepared by the Monticello staff, this guidebook is
dedicated to all those who visit Thomas Jefferson's beloved
home, and to all others with an interest in Jefferson and his
lasting influence around the world.

DANIEL P. JORDAN

About the Foundation

On April 13, 1923, the 180th anniversary of Thomas Jefferson's birth, the Thomas Jefferson Memorial Foundation, Inc. (now the Thomas Jefferson Foundation, Inc.), was chartered in New York City with the goal of purchasing and preserving Monticello as a national monument.

The Trustees of the Foundation purchased the estate, then consisting of the house and 600 acres (now almost 2,000) for $500,000 from Jefferson Monroe Levy, whose family had owned and preserved Monticello for most of the century following Jefferson's death. A national fundraising drive, which included a "pennies for Monticello" effort by schoolchildren, collected money for the purchase. Title came with the payment of $100,000 in cash, and on December 1, 1923, the Foundation assumed ownership and operational control.

Headed by Stuart Gibboney, a native Virginian and successful New York attorney, the Trustees took up the enormous tasks of paying the mortgage, maintaining the property, and restoring the house and gardens. Over the years, original furnishings have been patiently collected by loan, gift, and purchase, so that today, the house appears much as Jefferson knew it.

Between 1939 and 1941 the Garden Club of Virginia revived the gardens on the west and east fronts with remarkable accuracy, laying the groundwork for continued scholarly restoration of Jefferson's gardens and landscape. In 1954, the house was structurally renovated, and the Foundation subsequently added educational programs to its primary mission of preservation. Today, the Foundation remains dedicated to those same purposes—preserving the finite resource that is Monticello, and sharing what is known about Thomas Jefferson, his world, and his legacy.

Preservation

Preserving Monticello is the combined responsibility of several Foundation departments: archaeology, buildings, curatorial, gardens and grounds, research, and restoration. They work together to maintain the house and landscape, as well as to conduct research and to carry out special projects. An example of this team approach is the replacement of Monticello's complex roof in 1992, a project which restored Jefferson's innovative design, materials, and technology, while preventing the roof's perennial leaks. This monumental undertaking earned the Foundation several honors, including the first-ever Award of Excellence in the Stewardship of Historic Sites from the National Trust for Historic Preservation.

Preservation at Monticello is ongoing. Recent projects saw the upgrading of the heating, ventilating, and air conditioning system for the house; cleaning and repair of the Great Clock in the Entrance Hall; and maintenance work on the double-acting doors. Important restoration initiatives on the grounds include the re-establishment of Monticello's 1,000-foot vegetable garden and the recreation of Jefferson's plant nursery, grove, fruit orchards, and vineyards. The road by which most of the 550,000 annual visitors approach Monticello is being transformed into the Thomas Jefferson Parkway, offering a protected and scenic linear park with an arboretum, hiking and biking trails, and open vistas to the Blue Ridge Mountains.

Education

Outreach is the other part of the Foundation's mission. Ongoing programs include year-round guided tours of the house, as well as guided tours of the gardens and the slave sites along Mulberry Row in warmer months. In addition,

Garden tours of Monticello guide 33,000 visitors through the landscape every year.

the Monticello education department interprets the house and grounds in special programs for more than 12,000 students each year. The department also sponsors summer camps for elementary students, after-school programs, and weekend child-parent activities. Twice a year, senior citizens from across the country gather in Charlottesville for a week-long Elderhostel program focusing on Jefferson. Other classes include summer seminars for history teachers, an archaeological field school, a historic landscape institute, and a course on Jefferson and Monticello taught by Monticello staff members, all offered through the University of Virginia.

The Foundation provides numerous other educational programs. Together with the Foundation's Thomas Jefferson Center for Historic Plants, Monticello's gardens and grounds staff sponsors workshops, lectures, and natural history walks through their "Saturdays in the Gardens" series. Slavery at Monticello is interpreted through guided tours of Mulberry Row, summer demonstrations of plantation crafts and skills, public programs, and publications.

Monticello staff members lecture frequently, at conferences and for various organizations coast to coast.

The Foundation's publications program includes original monographs and reprints of classic Jefferson titles. The department of public affairs publishes a newsletter, *Monticello,* and the Center for Historic Plants distributes one called *Twinleaf.*

Computer users worldwide can access the Foundation's Web site at **http://www.monticello.org**. Students of Jefferson can acquire products and books relating to him, his interests, and his era at the Monticello museum shops or through the Monticello catalog.

Studying Jefferson and his legacy is a major part of the Foundation's educational mission. The International Center for Jefferson Studies oversees the scholarly activities of the Foundation, including the departments of archaeology, education, and research. The International Center, established in partnership with the University of Virginia, encourages the study and teaching of Jefferson by sponsoring publications and lectures, hosting visiting researchers and interns, and organizing conferences and seminars for scholars, teachers, and museum professionals.

Slavery is one area of current Foundation research. A major undertaking is *Getting Word,* an oral history project in which staff members interview the descendants of Monticello slaves.

Special Programs

Monticello is open to the public every day except Christmas and has an active calendar of special events. These include the celebration of Jefferson's birth on April 13 and winter programs, such as wreath making and

Demonstration of textile skills on Plantation Community weekend.

evening tours in December. Every July Fourth, a Federal District Court convenes on the West Lawn of Monticello for a naturalization ceremony, at which dozens of people become American citizens. In cooperation with the University of Virginia, the Foundation annually awards medals to leaders in law and architecture, fields that Jefferson himself advanced.

The importance of Jefferson's home, architecturally and symbolically, is recognized worldwide. In the last decade alone, more than twenty heads of state, including Mikhail Gorbachev, the Emperor and Empress of Japan, Lady Margaret Thatcher, and four U.S. Presidents, have come to the mountaintop to pay their respects to the "architect of democracy."

In addition to revenue from ticket sales and museum shops, Monticello's mission of education and preservation is supported by the work of its development program, established in 1989. The Foundation's first fundraising campaign since the drive to purchase Monticello in the 1920s—supporting educational programs, funding preservation projects, and establishing a permanent endowment—was completed in 1996.

For more information about the private, nonprofit Thomas Jefferson Foundation or about how to support its work, please write: P.O. Box 217, Charlottesville, Virginia, 22902.

Monticello After Jefferson

1827	Public auction of Jefferson's slaves and household furnishings at Monticello.
1831	Monticello purchased by James T. Barclay.
1834	Monticello purchased by Uriah P. Levy, United States Navy.
1862–1879	Monticello's ownership under litigation.
1879	Jefferson Monroe Levy acquired Monticello.
1923	Thomas Jefferson Memorial Foundation purchased Monticello. Campaign begun to pay off mortgage and acquire objects.
1937–1941	Substantial restoration and reconstruction of the house and grounds, including the North and South Dependencies, and the East and West Lawn gardens.
1953–54	Structural renovations of the house undertaken, and a central heating and air-conditioning system installed.
1978	First planting in the recreated Grove.
1979–present	Ongoing archaeological excavations of landscape features, Mulberry Row, and sites associated with free and enslaved workers.
1981	1,000-foot-long garden wall reconstructed.

East Front, perhaps 1870.

Monticello after Jefferson

1982	First trees planted in recreated South Orchard.
1984	Garden Pavilion reconstructed.
1985	Commemoration of Levy family contributions.
1986	Visitor Center exhibition and facility opened. Education department established.
1987	Center for Historic Plants established. Monticello named to World Heritage List.
1989	Historic State Dinner for U.S. President Bush and 53 Governors.
1991-92	House roof restoration.
1991-95	Archaeological excavations at Shadwell.
1993	Commemoration of 250th Anniversary of Jefferson's birth. Loan exhibition "The Worlds of Thomas Jefferson at Monticello." Oral history project on descendants of Monticello slaves begun.
1995	International Center for Jefferson Studies dedicated.
1996	"The Jefferson Moment" comprehensive campaign completed. Thomas Jefferson Parkway groundbreaking.

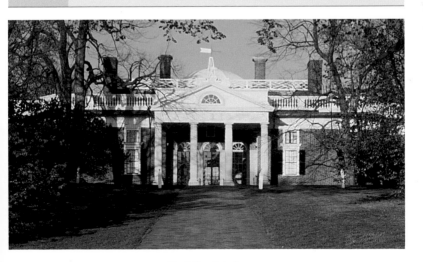

East Front, today.

Suggested Further Reading

What follows is a highly selective list. A much more extensive listing, "Books on Thomas Jefferson & Monticello," is available free from the Monticello Museum Shop, P. O. Box 316, Charlottesville, Virginia 22902.

On Monticello:
William Howard Adams, *Jefferson's Monticello* (1983)
Jack McLaughlin, *Jefferson and Monticello: The Biography of a Builder* (1988)
Susan R. Stein, *The Worlds of Thomas Jefferson at Monticello* (1993)

Biographical Works:
Noble E. Cunningham, Jr., *In Pursuit of Reason: The Life of Thomas Jefferson* (1987)
Dumas Malone, *Jefferson and His Time,* 6 volumes (1948-81)
Dumas Malone, *Thomas Jefferson: A Brief Biography* (1993)
Merrill D. Peterson, *Thomas Jefferson and the New Nation* (1970)
Sarah N. Randolph, *The Domestic Life of Thomas Jefferson* (1871: rept. 1985)

Jefferson's Writings:
Edwin M. Betts, ed., *Thomas Jefferson's Farm Book* (1953; rept. 1976)
Edwin M. Betts, ed., *Thomas Jefferson's Garden Book* (1944; rept. 1985)
Edwin M. Betts and James A. Bear, Jr., eds., *The Family Letters of Thomas Jefferson* (1966; rept. 1985)
Julian P. Boyd and others, eds., *The Papers of Thomas Jefferson,* 27 volumes (1950)
Lester J. Cappon, ed., *The Adams-Jefferson Letters* (1959; rept. 1987)
Bernard Mayo, ed., *Jefferson Himself,* (1942; rept. 1970)
Merrill D. Peterson, ed., *Thomas Jefferson: Writings* (1984)

James Morton Smith, ed., *The Republic of Letters: The Correspondence between Thomas Jefferson and James Madison 1776-1826* (1995)

On Jefferson's Political Thought and Legacy:

Joseph J. Ellis, *American Sphinx: The Character of Thomas Jefferson* (1997)

Adrienne Koch, *The Philosophy of Thomas Jefferson* (1943)

Richard Matthews, *The Radical Politics of Thomas Jefferson* (1986)

Peter S. Onuf, ed., *Jeffersonian Legacies* (1993)

Merrill D. Peterson, *The Jefferson Image in the American Mind* (1960)

Robert W. Tucker and David C. Hendrickson, *Empire of Liberty: The Statecraft of Thomas Jefferson* (1990)

Garry Wills, *Inventing America: Jefferson's Declaration of Independence* (1978)

Jefferson's Interests and Special Topics:

Dickinson W. Adams, ed., *Jefferson's Extracts from the Gospels* (1983)

William Howard Adams, ed., *Jefferson and the Arts: An Extended View* (1976)

James A. Bear, Jr., ed., *Jefferson at Monticello* (1967)

Silvio A. Bedini, *Thomas Jefferson: Statesman of Science* (1990)

Edwin M. Betts and Hazlehurst Bolton Perkins, *Thomas Jefferson's Flower Garden at Monticello*, 3d edition (1986)

Andrew Burstein, *The Inner Jefferson: Portrait of a Grieving Optimist* (1995)

Helen C. Cripe, *Thomas Jefferson and Music* (1974)

Frank L. Dewey, *Thomas Jefferson Lawyer* (1986)

Edwin S. Gaustad, *Sworn on the Altar of God: A Religious Biography of Thomas Jefferson* (1996)

Peter J. Hatch, *The Gardens of Monticello* (1992)

Donald Jackson, *Thomas Jefferson and the Stony Mountains:
Exploring the West from Monticello* (1981)

Marie Kimball, *Thomas Jefferson's Cook Book* (1949: rept. 1987)

Karl Lehmann, *Thomas Jefferson American Humanist* (1947)

Howard C. Rice, *Thomas Jefferson's Paris* (1976)

George Green Shackelford, *Thomas Jefferson's Travels in Europe
1784-1789* (1995)

Bernard W. Sheehan, *Seeds of Extinction: Jeffersonian
Philanthropy and the American Indian* (1973)

Herbert E. Sloan, *Principle and Interest: Thomas Jefferson and the
Problem of Debt* (1995)

Lucia Stanton, *Slavery At Monticello* (1996)

Douglas L. Wilson, *Jefferson's Books* (1996)

Jefferson Bibliography:

Frank Shuffelton, *Thomas Jefferson: A Comprehensive Annotated
Bibliography of Writings About Him 1826-1980* (1983)

Frank Shuffelton, *Thomas Jefferson, 1981-1990: An Annotated
Bibliography* (1992)

Children's Books:

Natalie S. Bober, *Thomas Jefferson: Man on a Mountain* (1988)

Ruth Crisman, *Thomas Jefferson: A Man with a Vision* (1992)

Robin H. Gabriel and Dick Ruehrwein, *Discover Jefferson at
Monticello* (1989)

Milton Meltzer, *Thomas Jefferson: The Revolutionary
Aristocrat* (1991)

Russell Shorto, *Thomas Jefferson and the American Ideal* (1987)

CREDITS AND PERMISSIONS

Designed by Gibson Design Associates, Charlottesville, Virginia